The Charismatic Illusion

Expanded Revision of *The Charismatic Phenomenon*
with Answers to Questions

Peter Masters
and John C. Whitcomb

THE WAKEMAN TRUST, LONDON

THE CHARISMATIC ILLUSION
Expanded Revision of *The Charismatic Phenomenon*
with Answers to Questions

© Peter Masters & John C. Whitcomb 1982
This revised edition 2016

THE WAKEMAN TRUST
(Wakeman Trust is a UK Registered Charity)

Wakeman Trust UK Registered Office
38 Walcot Square
London SE11 4TZ

Wakeman Trust USA Office
300 Artino Drive
Oberlin, OH 44074-1263

Website: www.wakemantrust.org

ISBN 978 1 908919 70 0

Cover design by Andrew Owen
Cover image: Bigstockphoto.com

Printed by Stephens & George, Merthyr Tydfil, UK

Contents

The Illusion Introduced

S INCE THE HOLY SPIRIT came down on the newly-formed Church of Jesus Christ on the Day of Pentecost, two thousand years of Christian witness have passed, and momentous battles have been fought between the devil and the Church. Satan has launched brutal physical persecutions from without, and by infiltration has campaigned to overthrow evangelical doctrine from within. But, by the mighty power of the Spirit, a true Church – made up of myriad living congregations throughout the world – has prevailed and grown.

The history of the Church is studded with countless triumphs of grace, seen in mighty awakenings and periods when the wonderful light of God has streamed from his unchanging and inerrant Word. Yet all these glorious events of the Spirit have occurred, including all the battles of persecution, reformation and revival, without the benefit of the charismatic movement.

Pentecostalism began only towards the end of the 19th century, and never became more than a tiny part of the Christian witness scene for the first fifty years of its existence. The modern charismatic movement did not even begin to emerge from Pentecostalism until around 1955. At the present time it has existed for barely 60 years of the nearly 2,000 years which have elapsed since Pentecost.

For all this, charismatic teachers and authors are undaunted in their claim to have rediscovered the lost doctrines of the Spirit. They contemptuously sweep aside the witness of the centuries as a witness conducted in semi-darkness, coldness and powerlessness. Many of them say that there was no real worship until the charismatic movement came along – not for two millennia! Some assert that Christ's people have had their basic spiritual rights and blessings denied them for all these centuries because wicked generations of ministers, in order to sustain their elitist power and dominance, suppressed the facts about the gifts which should have been exercised and enjoyed by everyone. With such ideas as these, charismatics deride the age of the Spirit as an extended dark age of lifeless formalism. It is claimed that an ugly breach occurred in the spiritual life of God's people, extending from the close of the book of *Acts* until after 1955, when light and power broke forth again in the tongues and visions of charismatic pioneers.

The idea is chilling; the implications staggering. Is the charismatic movement a rediscovery of authentic Christianity? Has the genuine article really been missed by the great instruments of reformation and revival in ages past? Have all the sermons preached and hymns written over a period of 2,000 years been composed in the shadows of an age of spiritual ignorance? Has all the worship of these past years been void of vital life and power? Have numerous lifetimes of devoted labour been sacrificed on the altar of an inadequate and partial faith?

It has been said that the doctrines of the charismatic movement are either *true*, in which case the last 1,900 years have been an age of tragic spiritual deprivation, or these doctrines are *false*, and the manifestations illusory, in which case they represent a message of monumental arrogance, decrying the faith and experience of generations of spiritual forebears.

There have, we know, been some extremely rare and isolated incidents of phenomena corresponding to present-day charismatic experiences, but these are so few as to be statistically irrelevant in the history of the

Church of Christ. However, they are eagerly clutched at by charismatic authors anxious to convince their readers that the 'gifts' of the Spirit have always been manifested. But these writers know perfectly well that their use of history is slick and unethical. They build an Empire State Building out of two or three small bricks, shamelessly misleading their readers with ludicrous exaggerations and generalisations. The incontrovertible fact is that the history of the Church of Christ – the age of the Spirit – has proceeded for the most part without the charismatic movement.

As we have already indicated, it was around 1955 that Pentecostal doctrines began to spread out into other denominations. At first, this occurred extremely slowly, but in April 1960 the rector of an Episcopal church in California announced to his congregation that he had received the baptism of the Spirit and spoken in tongues. This event, which attracted widespread television and newspaper coverage in the USA and gave rise to a best-selling book, is often cited as the effective launching of the modern charismatic movement.

At first, the movement spread rapidly among people with a fairly loose hold on evangelical doctrines, appealing also to many liberals and Catholics. Interestingly, the first crop of societies set up for the promotion of charismatic gifts made it their declared aim to employ the 'gifts of the Spirit' as a means of joining all Christians together in a united Christian front. The overwhelming majority of charismatic leaders still hope for a worldwide ecumenical church under the leadership of the pope. The charismatic movement has certainly spread extensively within the Roman Catholic Church. However, while vast numbers of priests now employ charismatic jargon and methods of worship, their Catholic doctrines remain totally unchanged. In developing countries the charismatic movement has seen quite phenomenal expansion, but the kind of churches which have sprung into being often resemble cult meetings much more than Christian churches.

Alongside all the extremism and all the excesses, it must be recognised that the charismatic movement includes many people who are genuine and earnest disciples of the Lord. Equally there are some charismatic fellowships which remain untainted by the worldliness, shallowness,

gimmickry and phoney claims which characterise charismatics generally. Nevertheless, even in these better groups, charismatic practices are
a great and serious departure from the Bible which will greatly injure
true believers, conditioning them for the worse excesses and extremes
which are coming in like an irresistible tide.

We cannot be vague or indifferent in our attitude to charismatic
claims, and it is hoped that the points raised in this book will help
many friends to examine the movement in the light of our only source
of guidance for spiritual matters – God's perfect and infallible Word.

1
The Longing for Signs and Wonders

THE CHARISMATIC PHENOMENA which we are witnessing today can be explained by virtue of the widespread scepticism and denial of the Truth in the world around us. God and his attributes and works are denied because of rationalistic, evolutionary, materialistic and atheistic thinking, and in such a world the churches are under tremendous pressure to demonstrate somehow to an unbelieving society that God is alive, that he has power and wisdom, and that he really did do all the mighty miracles and signs which are recorded in his Word.

This is the frame of reference, the atmosphere, which has given rise to the desperate danger we face today, namely the desire to force God to give us (or to conjure up for ourselves) demonstrations of power which will convince ourselves and others that God is indeed the God of Holy Scripture. We have examples in the Bible of times when God's people of old felt a similar desire for a public vindication of their God. The desire was legitimate and worthy, but was never answered by God. Prayers – desperate cries – were made for visible sign-miracles, but they were never given to satisfy the desire of God's people.

An example of this is recorded in *Isaiah 64*. Isaiah was probably the greatest of the writing prophets of the Old Testament, a man who struggled against the scepticism of King Ahaz and against all false worship and occultism (as described in *Isaiah 8*). In his heart, he longed for some visible, genuine, spectacular vindication of the one, true, living God of Israel. Follow his prayer carefully: 'Oh that thou wouldest rend the heavens, that thou wouldest come down, that the mountains might flow down at thy presence, as when the melting fire burneth, the fire causeth the waters to boil, to make thy name known to thine adversaries, that the nations may tremble at thy presence!'

Was this a legitimate prayer? Of course it was! He wanted his God vindicated before an apostate, sceptical, unbelieving, hard-hearted nation and world. Furthermore, Isaiah had a precedent to quote, for 700 years earlier God had done something like this. So, Isaiah pleaded – 'When thou didst terrible things which we looked not for, thou camest down, the mountains flowed down at thy presence' *(Isaiah 64.3)*.

At the Exodus, and at Sinai, God had publicly vindicated his servant Moses in the eyes of Israel and of Egypt and of all the nations of the world. There had been an absolutely spectacular combination of sign-miracles to such an extent that when Mount Sinai was shaken by the power of God and smoked as a furnace and a great voice was heard, the nation cried out in terror.

Nevertheless, Isaiah's prayer for a new exhibition of God's power went unanswered. He never saw that type of public, spectacular display – apart from the reversal of the shadow on the sundial during the reign of Hezekiah. The Lord knows what he is doing, when he is going to do it, and how he is going to accomplish it. The visible vindication of God is never according to our human desires, suggestions or schemes. It is entirely according to God's sovereign will.

In *Acts 1.6* we read of how the disciples confronted the Lord with this urgent question – 'Lord, wilt thou at this time restore again the kingdom to Israel?' Our Lord's answer to them echoes to this very hour – 'It is not for you to know the times or the seasons, which the Father hath put in his own power.' Their task was simply to obey the immediate instructions of the great commission, and to leave the programme, the plan, the chronology, the timing of the introduction of the kingdom and the public vindication of God to him.

Today we have a situation which is very similar to the desperate cry of Isaiah (later echoed by John the Baptist). It is this – 'Lord, please do something *now*! Look at the state of the churches – look at the decline, look at the humiliation of thy people today in contrast to the great evidences of blessing in centuries gone by. Do something to vindicate thy servants, Lord.'

Every major cult and false form of Christianity is offering miracles to its followers in order to vindicate its testimony in an unbelieving world. The rapid growth of cults can be put down to this – the built-in guarantee that people will feel, experience and see visible, public, spectacular vindications of God. So, great and almost irresistible pressure is placed on God's people today to desire some spectacular vindication. Many look at the Bible and say, 'But isn't the Bible just full of sign-miracles? Why is it that people in those days could experience and perform miracles and we cannot?'

The Bible, however, is not 'full' of sign-miracles in the sense of their being continuous. We must never forget that a careful analysis of the Bible shows that miracles did not happen every other week to every other person. They were, in fact, among the rarest events in the history of the world. Any Bible student who takes time to trace through Bible history will discover that from the time of the creation of the world to the Flood nearly 1,700 years later, there was only one sign-miracle recorded, and that was the translation of Enoch without dying into the presence of the Lord. Of course, in the final phase of this period there was the ark-building project, but from outward observation even that was not a sign-miracle.

From the Flood to the time of the patriarchs, there was also only one sign-miracle – the judgement of the Tower of Babel. And from the time of the patriarchs down to Moses, sign-miracles were very rare. Then, through four hundred years of bondage in Egypt there was not one word from Heaven, nor a single sign-miracle. Suddenly, there came the great outburst of miraculous signs in the time of Moses and Joshua. Throughout the crisis of the Exodus and the Conquest there were many, becoming more spasmodic in the time of the Judges. Later, the sign-miracles became very rare once again, and there were none in the time of Solomon.

In the period of the divided monarchy from Solomon all the way down to Nehemiah, sign-miracles were so rare as to be practically non-existent. There were, of course, exceptions. Elijah and Elisha experienced sign-miracles, and Jonah figured in a great messianic sign. But set against five centuries, the signs were very few. Some of the godliest men in that period of history, such as Ezra, Nehemiah and Zerubbabel, never experienced one sign-miracle. When the Old Testament period as such came to a conclusion, there followed a 400-year period (until the time of John the Baptist) which is traditionally known as the period of God's silence. Many interesting things were happening, but there was not one sign-miracle, and no voice from Heaven.

Even more amazing is the fact that when we come to John the Baptist, though he was the greatest prophet that ever lived, the Scripture insists that John never performed one sign-miracle in his whole life *(John 10.41)*. If this is an amazing reflection, what about the Lord Jesus himself? He was the greatest miracle-worker, and the Son of the living God, yet he did not perform one miracle for the first thirty years of his life.

Some early Christians were so shocked and offended by the statement in *John 2.11* informing us that the changing of water into wine was the first miracle Jesus ever performed, that they foolishly accepted apocryphal gospels filled with fictional details of sign-miracles which Jesus performed when he was a child and a teenager. They felt a need to fill in the supposed void and to alleviate the intense embarrassment of having the Son of God performing no sign-miracles for thirty years.

Why did the Lord perform no miracle in all those years? It is probably because sign-miracles increase in their value in exact proportion to their rarity. If they had happened constantly and in response to anyone's request or need, they would soon have become commonplace and lost their dynamic, revelatory value. God wisely limited his signs, and so people could not predict when, how or where he would do such things.

Also our God very wisely, and for obvious reasons, eliminated all miracle-working competition from around his beloved Son. Even his own forerunner John the Baptist worked no sign-miracles in order that special attention should be focused on the claims of the Lord Jesus before the nation of Israel. The Old Testament had said over and over again that when the Messiah came, they would know who he was because of his sign-miracles.

2
Testing Today's Miracles

A S WE TRACE through the New Testament we see the precise reason why our Lord Jesus Christ performed his sign-miracles. He did *not* perform spectacular sign-miracles merely in order to demonstrate to Israel that there was a living God in Heaven who could perform miracles. The Israelites already knew that, because they had been in possession of their Scriptures for hundreds of years and knew all about the character and power of God. That was *not* the reason.

Nor did Jesus perform sign-miracles solely to help people feel better if they were sick, or become whole and healthy if they were crippled. Our Lord explained why he did his miracles. The signs were performed – 'that ye might believe that Jesus is the Christ, the Son of God'. In *Acts 2.22* the apostles confirmed that Jesus Christ was proved to be the Messiah sent from God by the sign-miracles which he performed.

The Lord Jesus absolutely devastated all charges that he was a false prophet by two things: first, he spoke in accordance with Scripture, in complete harmony with previous revelation; and secondly he made prophecies about sign-miracles that he himself proceeded to fulfil.

We see the purpose which lay behind our Lord's miracles in the healing of the paralytic recorded in *Matthew 9.2-8*. As the scene opens, a hopeless cripple is being brought to Jesus by friends. Jesus, seeing their faith, said to the paralytic, 'Son, be of good cheer; thy sins be forgiven thee.' The enemies of Jesus immediately saw this as utter blasphemy. How could a mere finite, sinful man forgive the sins of another human being? Of course, if Jesus had indeed been finite and sinful then their opinion would have been correct. But Jesus, knowing their thoughts, said, 'Wherefore think ye evil in your hearts? For whether is easier, to say, Thy sins be forgiven thee; or to say, Arise, and walk?'

If Jesus had not truly been the Son of God, the worst possible thing for him to have done in the presence of a hostile audience would have been to look at a hopeless cripple and say, 'Arise, and walk.' But he did just this, saying – 'But that ye may know that the Son of man hath power on earth to forgive sins...Arise, take up thy bed, and go unto thine house...But when the multitudes saw it, they marvelled, and glorified God.'

The sign-miracle of the instantaneous and perfect healing of the paralytic convinced the multitude that what Jesus had said concerning this man's sins was true – he had been forgiven. The sign-miracle confirmed his power and authority to do the greater thing, namely, to deal with sin. Thus the sign-miracle accomplished *not* a demonstration that God exists; nor the helping of a poor cripple; but the sign-miracle chiefly called attention to Christ's unique authority on earth to forgive sin.

We must grasp this essential principle – the message which goes with the sign-miracle is all-important. If a sign-miracle ever occurred without having a divine purpose or message attached to it, it would be a total disaster.

It is recorded in *Acts 14* that when Paul and Barnabas came to the town of Lystra, they found a crippled man outside the city, and they determined in the name of Jesus Christ to heal him. But before they had an opportunity to explain who they were, and who their God was, the whole city was electrified by the event and rushed out (under the leadership of pagan priests) to offer sacrifices to these two men. The people considered them gods, giving them the names of mythical, pagan gods.

Were Paul and Barnabas pleased to be honoured in this way? No, they rent their garments and cried out in alarm. What went wrong was this: the sign-miracle had become separated from the message, and so disaster and misunderstanding resulted. This is precisely what is happening today. Hundreds of thousands of professing Christians want sign-miracles in order to vindicate both God and themselves before an unbelieving world. But if there is no supernatural revelation with the signs they become a disaster. A miracle in itself is worse than nothing, unless God, by the miracle, is indicating who the *messenger* is and what the *purpose* really is.

Many of God's people who have a deep desire to honour him are inclined to believe that he is again speaking in special ways, and certain people are attracting great attention as they perform sign-miracles in support of their messages. By what test can we determine whether they really are receiving new insights directly from God – that is, by means other than the prayerful, careful, systematic study of Scripture?

How can we know whether their so-called sign-miracles are indeed from God or from some other source? We have in the Scripture guidelines which are very simple and available and which are appropriate for all God's people to use. Using these guidelines we can obey *1 John 4.1* – 'Beloved, believe not every spirit, but try the spirits whether they are of God.'

What are these guidelines? How can we test the miracles of physical healing which every major cult including Roman Catholicism specialises in? How can we determine whether these so-called healings are on the same level and just as genuine as the miracles of healing which we find in the New Testament? Here are three guidelines from the Scriptures. It is by these 'standards' that we must judge all claims to sign-miracles today:–

(1) The healing miracles of our Lord Jesus Christ were extraordinarily abundant in number.

(2) The healing ministry of our Lord Jesus Christ included *spectacular* healings. They involved dramatic organic and physical restoration which was highly visible and obvious to all.

Now of course, today we have many claims that people have been healed of internal aches and pains, but it is very difficult in most cases for the average person to be sure whether or not a healing has actually taken place. Our Lord specialised in the kind of healing miracle which was obvious and spectacular. For example, in the Garden of Gethsemane the sole contribution of the apostle Peter to the crisis of the hour was to remove an ear from the servant of the high priest. The Lord Jesus picked up the severed ear, put it back in place, and completely healed the wound. Can miracle-workers today achieve the kind of healing that Jesus performed? Of course not.

Jesus was able to heal a man born blind, and the man said, 'Since the world began was it not heard that any man opened the eyes of one that was born blind.' What would happen if one took the body of a loved one who had recently died to a charismatic healer and asked that person to do what Jesus did for Lazarus? We may be sure that no healer would look at such a case and endanger their reputation by attempting to do what they know is altogether impossible. The excuse which 'healers' make today for failing to achieve mighty healings is that the people have no faith, but in the New Testament faith did not necessarily have anything to do with these spectacular healings. Nine out of the ten hopeless lepers whom Jesus healed apparently had no faith. Only one was a believer who came back to thank his Lord. It seems fairly obvious that Lazarus did not need to exercise faith to be raised from the dead. So we may be sure that the complaint about smallness of faith in the 'client' is simply a modern excuse or a cover-up for the fact that these sign-miracles of the Scripture are not being duplicated today.

(3) The most important guideline of all is this: when the Son of God performed miraculous healings to authenticate his claim to be Israel's Messiah, he did so in such a way that no one could deny that a miracle of God had taken place. His sign-miracles were undeniable. Nicodemus came to him one night and put it this way – 'We know that thou art a teacher come from God: for no man can do these miracles that thou doest, except God be with him' *(John 3.2)*.

Some of the Lord's enemies who recognised that the miracles were genuine and that people actually were healed and raised from the dead, were forced to claim that Satan was the one who did all these things.

But all were compelled to agree that mighty, spectacular, undeniable miracles occurred. The only debate left was – what supernatural power is the cause, God or the devil?

We read in *John 11.47* that the chief priests and Pharisees gathered in a council and acknowledged that they did not know how to oppose Christ, because he definitely did many miracles. That is echoed in *Acts 4.16* when another Jewish council considered the miracle wrought by Peter and John in healing a paralytic in the Temple. The Jewish leaders said among themselves: 'What shall we do to these men? for that indeed a notable miracle hath been done by them is manifest to all them that dwell in Jerusalem; and we cannot deny it.' Whenever God involves himself in sign-miracles they are always completely *undeniable*. On Mount Carmel, Elijah, in the name of the true God of Israel, performed a miracle that was totally undeniable. After the fire fell from Heaven, no one asked, 'Did it really happen?' Similarly in Egypt the great plagues leading up to the Exodus forced the magicians to recognise, 'This is the finger of God.'

On the basis of these considerations, I place before readers an infallible measuring stick by which to determine whether or not sign-miracles are really happening today. If anyone can observe these miracles and remain sceptical, then they are nothing like the sign-miracles of the Bible and the 'miracle-worker' cannot be from God. This single test demolishes all present-day claims to validity on the part of miracle-workers. God cannot possibly be the author of sign-miracles which can be denied. A comparison of the works of the Lord Jesus and his appointed apostles with the works performed today by charismatic miracle-workers will reveal a stupendous difference. We are looking at two entirely different levels of reality.

3
What Are the Greater Works?

THE MODERN TREND of demanding miracles of healing and claiming to have experienced them, demonstrates a complete misunderstanding of the key Bible passage in this whole matter – *John 14.12*. In this passage we read the promise given by the Lord in the upper room the night before he died. Once Judas Iscariot had departed from their midst, leaving eleven true disciples, the Lord Jesus said these profound words – 'Verily, verily, I say unto you, He that believeth on me, the works that I do shall he do also.'

The eleven disciples did do sign-miracles as Jesus had done, even raising the dead. But now listen to the second phase of the promise, and it is this phase which applies particularly to us – 'and greater works than these shall he do; because I go unto my Father.' Think how great our Lord's works were! They were undeniable and spectacular. He changed water to wine – performing an instantaneous creation-miracle producing a highly complex biochemical end-product, possessing the appearance of a 'history' it did not have. He multiplied loaves and fishes, thousands of them, with an appearance of a 'history' not one of them had.

Think of the spectacular healings of hopeless lepers, cripples and blind people. Remember that every one of these sign-miracles had an intentional, God-designed, built-in limitation. The water which was changed to wine solved a wedding crisis but it was apparently the last time that such a thing was ever done. No other wedding in Galilee facing a similar problem would ever receive that kind of help again. In other words, Jesus did not permanently solve that kind of problem in Galilee, and he did not intend to.

Our Lord fed five thousand men on one occasion and four thousand on another, but in so doing he had no intention of solving the food problem in Galilee. He never planned to. The Lord Jesus healed tens of thousands of people, but we must remember the full truth about those people whom he healed. Every single one of them died anyway. In other words, he did not permanently solve the problem of their ageing and deterioration. He did not intend to. We may think of poor Lazarus, truly raised from the dead by the Lord Jesus, but when he came back from the dead, he knew he had to die again. He was restored to life with a mortal, sinful body like the one he first died with, because our Lord Jesus did not intend to permanently solve his death problem by that resuscitation.

When we think about these things, we begin to see what our Lord was implying when he said – 'Greater works than these shall he do.' There was clearly a work to be done which Jesus did not come to fully perform personally. His work was to pave the way for a *greater work* by the shedding of his precious blood and his resurrection from the dead. By his atoning death and resurrection he made it possible for us – his disciples – to do the greater work which is to take the revelation of God, the true Gospel of Jesus Christ, and to proclaim that message to the ends of the earth.

Every year since the work of Christ was completed thousands of people have heard the Gospel message and by the Spirit of God have believed it. Then a miracle has been performed within their sinful, darkened, spiritually deadened hearts. They have become alive for ever, a miracle which does not have to be repeated; a miracle which is a permanent solution to their every problem. When the Spirit of God entered in to take up his eternal dwelling within their souls, these people became a permanent part of the Body of Christ, eternally forgiven and saved.

Can we deny that this is a far greater work than that of temporary, physical healings or sign-miracles, great as they undoubtedly were in the physical realm? Miracle healings were only signs; they were never designed by God to be a complete, adequate solution to the real and deep problems of the human race. We see that God's programme for today has a dual purpose:–

(1) Through the *greater works* he is dealing with the spiritual catastrophe of man. Using the faithful, prayerful preaching of the Word of God in local churches, he works through soul-winners and witnessing Christians. This great mission is vastly more important than any claim we may hear about a physical sign-miracle. Such a sign-miracle in this age would be a downward, backward move compared to the greater things now happening through God's people.

(2) God's second purpose is to prepare us for the final phase of his redemptive work. Ultimately he is going to deal with our bodies also. Paul reminds us of God's purpose for these bodies of ours when he says, 'Ourselves also, which have the firstfruits of the Spirit … groan within ourselves, waiting for the adoption, to wit, the redemption of our body' *(Romans 8.23)*. Ultimately God will confirm our spiritual regeneration with a glorified, physical body when he raises us from the dead and we become perfect – when we see him as he is. Then all tears will be wiped away from our eyes, all suffering and pain will cease, all sin will be removed, and we will be in perfection before him for ever and ever as his servants, having none of the limitations which we now know.

God is preparing us for this, not by giving us instantaneous, spectacular healings to relieve pressure, suffering, inconvenience and discomfort. Today he is preparing us, by his grace, to be those who attract attention to Christ himself, not to *ourselves* – our claims, our experiences, and our healings. Let us exhort ourselves and our charismatic acquaintances to focus people upon Christ instead of ourselves. The ultimate tragedy of the charismatic movement is the tremendous emphasis on *me and my experience*, instead of Jesus Christ – his Word, his great commission, his promises, his programme, his timetable, his priorities. What the churches desperately need today is not some new formula for exorcism, or some new leader for faith-healing. It is not some new wave of tongues-speaking, or some weird serpent or poison ministry. Local churches of Christ need a renewed dedication to the infallible, inerrant, complete, sufficient, written revelation of God in Holy Scripture, preached in the power of the Holy Spirit and out of love for men and women in their lost condition.

4
Today's Gifts Are Not the Same

WHENEVER ANYONE enquires about the apparent 'gifts' being manifested in the charismatic movement, we need to point out that these gifts are nothing like the sign-gifts which were experienced by the apostles and churches of New Testament times. In those days speaking in tongues meant speaking in a real foreign language, never learned by the speaker, whereas now it means speaking in a strange, unheard-of language, claimed to be an ecstatic or even a heavenly language.

To defend the non-literal languages of today, many charismatic teachers refer to *1 Corinthians 13.1* where Paul uses the expression – 'Though I speak with the tongues of men and of angels'. This, they claim, confirms that tongues-speaking includes heavenly or angelic utterances. But this is obviously a mistaken interpretation because Paul is using hyperbole or exaggeration to make a point. He says – 'Though I speak with the tongues of men and of angels, and have not charity, I am become as sounding brass, or a tinkling cymbal.' He clearly means that even if we could do the impossible – speak angels' languages – a lack of love would demonstrate spiritual emptiness.

Paul uses the same method of argument repeatedly in these verses. He says, for example, that if he knew all mysteries and had all knowledge, and all faith, and could remove mountains, but lacked love, he would be nothing. It is obvious that no Christian will ever know everything while on earth, nor have total faith, which makes it clear that Paul is using hyperbole to express his point as forcefully as possible. It is very poor interpretation to wrench Paul's words out of their context and to use them in support of the idea that believers on earth may speak angelic tongues.

We may be certain that the tongues spoken in *Acts* were real foreign languages because foreigners could understand them *(Acts 2.6)*. We also know that the tongues-speaking discussed by Paul in *1 Corinthians* was the speaking of real foreign languages, because Paul says so, explaining that tongues-speaking is a fulfilment of a prophecy by Isaiah, that a time would come when Jews would be taught by God using Gentile languages *(Isaiah 28.11-12)*.

This was partly fulfilled when the Babylonians took the Jews into captivity, but Paul says that the complete fulfilment was the sign of tongues given to the Jews in New Testament times. Tongues were therefore real Gentile languages designed by God to strike awe into the hearts of doubtful and cynical Jews, and to show them that the new Christian church was from him.

It is significant that Luke, the inspired author of *Acts*, and Paul both use the same word for tongues. As companions, it is not possible that they would have used precisely the same term to describe totally different gifts, one being a real language, and the other a non-human, mysterious language. They would never have created such confusion, and neither would the Holy Spirit of Truth, the divine Author of the Scriptures.

We do occasionally hear the claim that someone has heard of a case in which a person spoke in a tongue which turned out to be the language of a remote nation or tribe, but such reports never seem to be substantiated by credible evidence. It appears that no charismatic gathering anywhere witnesses the amazing phenomenon of believers speaking in real, identifiable foreign languages which they have never learned, as in Bible times. Charismatics usually teach newcomers how to speak in tongues, often by repeating elementary sounds until the characteristic features of self-induced tongues develop.

In New Testament times real words were given by the Spirit, which the speakers themselves understood – as we shall prove later. At the same time a gift of interpretation was given to another person to corroborate the phenomenon. This manifestation of the Spirit's power was something which could not be counterfeited, and which stood up to cynical scrutiny.

The tongues spoken in *Acts* and *1 Corinthians* were real languages that accomplished God's purpose, which was to cause Jewish people deeply prejudiced against the Gospel to be confounded, and to marvel at the works of God *(Acts 2.6-7)*. While this sign could not produce saving faith, it provided challenging evidence of God's presence with the newly-formed Christian church, and warned that the period of Jewish privilege was at an end. Such tongues-speaking is not reported anywhere these days.

A charismatic classic from the early days of the movement – *The Holy Spirit and You,* by Dennis and Rita Bennett – shows just how far from the New Testament modern tongues-speaking is. The authors go as far as to say that many people have spoken in tongues without even knowing it. They write that when they told people about speaking in tongues, some would occasionally say, 'Oh, you mean that funny little language which I have spoken ever since I was a child, is that it? It makes me feel happy and close to God.'

The authors' confusion on the subject is also seen when they answer the question – What are we supposed to feel when we speak in tongues? They say: 'At first, you may feel nothing at all; remember this is not an emotional experience. You are trying to let your spirit have freedom to praise God as the Holy Spirit inspires. It may be a little while before your spirit can begin to break through to your feelings, giving you a new awareness of God within you. On the other hand, you may experience a sudden breakthrough, and feel as if you were carried right up into the heavenlies. You will say, "Praise the Lord!" It is wonderful to do that, to become suddenly aware of the fulness of Christ in you and to be carried up by it. Many people just sense a lightness and a reality down in their spirit as they begin to speak.'

However, while the Bennetts say that tongues-speaking is not an emotional experience, they describe it in purely emotional terms. They say nothing here about the tongue edifying or touching the understanding, or edifying the church, let alone convicting Jewish people, which was the principal purpose of the tongues according to *1 Corinthians 14.21-22*. The prophet Isaiah (quoted by Paul) had said that the phenomenon would be specifically for Israelites, and Paul makes plain that it would be a sign to them, to convince them that the new church was true.

The Bennetts also provide the telling example of a young pastor who was 'determined to receive the Holy Spirit'. They prayed that he would receive the fulness that he was seeking, and very soon he began to tremble very violently and then 'to speak beautifully in a new language. He continued for perhaps two or three minutes and then stopped.' The next day he telephoned to say that he had not received the desired blessing. Dennis Bennett records that he was on the verge of saying, 'Too bad; better luck next time,' when he felt that that would be foolish. Instead he said, 'Look here, my friend, I saw you tremble under the power of the Holy Spirit and I heard you speak beautifully in a language you do not know. I know you know the Lord Jesus as your Saviour, so this must have been the Holy Spirit. Stop doubting and start thanking the Lord for baptising you in the Holy Spirit.' An hour later the young minister telephoned again to say that he was 'riding high'. He said, 'When you told me to do that, I began to thank the Lord for baptising me in the Spirit and wow, the joy of the Lord hit me and I am now on cloud nine.'

Was this a genuine experience of New Testament tongues? By the standards of the New Testament we can only answer that it was not. The language was obviously not a real foreign language, it had no meaning, message, or interpretation, and there was no Jewish person present who needed the sign-authentication value of a tongue. It was an entirely emotional matter. So there is no reason to believe that this 'tongue' was anything different from that spoken in numerous non-Christian cults.

It was an emotional tongue experienced by someone who was wrongly convinced that this was God's way, and was very anxious to receive it.

Today's tongues, by contrast with those of New Testament times, have absolutely no authenticating quality. Being totally different from the original gifts, they are powerless to confirm that God is uniquely with his people. The people who spoke in tongues in Bible times had a gift which no unbeliever could imitate or equal, whereas the tongues performed by charismatic people today are no different from those found for centuries in non-Christian religions and cults.

Many charismatic tongues-speakers have no idea that their kind of tongues-speaking is regularly practised among groups of Buddhists, Hindus, Mormons, Muslims, Shintoists, spiritists and voodoo devotees. Going back a little in time the Irvingites, Jansenists and American Shakers, and many Quakers, also spoke in unidentifiable tongues just as charismatics do today. In recent years many Bible-denying liberals have taken up tongues-speaking, as have very many Roman Catholics.

A researcher writing for a prestigious American sociological institute, found tongues-speaking was practised by the Hudson Bay Eskimos, as well as by the priestesses of animistic jungle tribes in North Borneo. There is nothing uniquely authenticating in the kind of unreal 'languages' spoken today. Any number of non-Christian and anti-Christian religions can do it. Similarly the kind of healing that we get today in evangelical circles is no different than the healings carried on by countless heretical faith-healing groups. It is not healing of an infallible and uniquely authenticating kind, as in the New Testament.

Tongues-speaking of exactly the same kind as that experienced by charismatics has also occurred under the influence of LSD. We also read of a report by Carl Jung in which he describes a spiritualist medium who spoke in tongues 'fluently, rapidly and with charm. She spoke with bewildering naturalness, and when she had finished there passed over her face an incredible expression of ecstatic blessing.'

Some years ago newspapers carried a report of a school where the sixth-formers had been entertaining themselves by hypnotising one another. On being threatened by the headmaster with expulsion if anyone else was found in an hypnotic trance, they turned their attention to other strange phenomena, especially speaking in tongues. Apparently none were believing Christians, but they achieved tongues-speaking very successfully, and put on a number of performances for the press. So among cults, heretics, pagan religions of remote tribes, cynical sixth-formers and LSD imbibers, ecstatic tongues are easily accomplished, proving that there is nothing about it that uniquely authenticates the true church of Christ.

By contrast, the tongues of New Testament times could never be duplicated by unsaved people because they were not non-literal languages but *real ones*. Today's gifts are therefore completely different from those seen in the New Testament, and cannot be regarded as an authenticating sign of God.

5
The Purpose of the Gifts Has Changed

BECAUSE THE GIFTS are now so different, and are no longer astounding or unique to the churches of Christ, it is not surprising that new teaching has evolved to clothe them with a new purpose. Charismatic books give entirely different reasons for the gifts from those given in the New Testament. Paul taught (see page 26) that tongues were a sign to the Jews that God was with the church of Christ *(1 Corinthians 14.21-22)*. They were also a channel of inspired teaching, like prophecy, especially necessary while the New Testament was not yet given. But charismatic teachers have added to these purposes, asserting that they are also for private worship, for ecstatic experience, for an incomprehensible form of prayer to God, and as an evidence of Spirit baptism.

Having wandered far from scriptural teaching, the main writers in the movement contradict each other in explaining what goes on in tongues-speaking. Some say that it is God supernaturally communicating with the spirit of the tongues-speaker, even though the speaker does not personally understand what the tongue means. Others, however, say that it is an activity by which the tongues-speaker communicates with

God (again, even though he does not know what he is saying). In a public meeting, the interpretation will be God's reply.

Still other charismatic teachers sit on the fence and say – 'It may be God speaking to you, or it may be you speaking to God.' One leading writer says: 'The child of God is privileged to have speech with God, and no man understands this secret speech for it is the language of divinity. It is neither understood by the person, nor by the devil.' Naturally, if we do not know the meaning of our words it is difficult to know who is speaking to whom, let alone what is being said.

When the world's leading charismatic writers develop opposite ideas of what tongues-speaking is about, how can anyone feel that they have a biblical warrant for what they are teaching? In New Testament times there was no doubt about the meaning of the foreign languages, and that through them *God* was speaking. *Then* it was a real and verifiable language supernaturally given. *Now* it is incomprehensible and strange. *Then* it brought a message. *Now* it is used privately without the speaker having any idea what it means. *Then* it was an impressive sign. *Now* it is a strange and disturbing form of unintelligible speech which repels the majority of unbelievers and does nothing to authenticate the Gospel.

What about the charismatic argument that signs and wonders should continue today in order to impress unbelievers and bring them to faith in Christ? The short answer is that present-day signs and wonders are not the same and are simply not up to it, as we have seen already. They do not compare with New Testament tongues and healings. The purpose of the original signs was to authenticate a *new* message, a *new* church, and particularly to authenticate the apostles appointed by the Lord as witnesses of the resurrection and channels of new revelation.

Here are some of the scriptures which show that the healing wonders were exclusive to the apostolic band for their personal authentication:–

'And by the hands of the apostles were many signs and wonders wrought among the people' *(Acts 5.12).*

'By word and deed, through mighty signs and wonders, by the power of the Spirit of God; so that from Jerusalem, and round about unto Illyricum, I have fully preached the gospel of Christ' (Paul, writing in *Romans 15.18-19).*

'Truly the signs of an apostle were wrought among you in all patience, in signs, and wonders, and mighty deeds' *(2 Corinthians 12.12).*

'How shall we escape, if we neglect so great salvation; which at the first began to be spoken by the Lord, and was confirmed unto us by them that heard him *[the apostles]*; God also bearing them witness, both with signs and wonders, and with divers miracles, and gifts of the Holy Ghost, according to his own will?' *(Hebrews 2.3-4.)*

We note that in this last passage the Word of God is already putting the signs and wonders into the past tense. This can only mean that the people were being taught to grasp that signs were already dying out because they had been designed only to give *initial* authentication to the New Testament apostles and the New Testament age. In *Hebrews 2* the New Testament is itself beginning to look back and say, 'Don't forget the signs and wonders which authenticated and identified the apostles. Remember how they underlined the fact that they were speaking from God.'

The charismatic movement has made an elementary and grave mistake in assuming that signs and wonders effected by the hands of gifted people were meant to continue down the centuries in order to create and sustain faith. Faith cannot be nourished on the miraculous. Indeed the reverse is true, for if true believers learn to depend on miracles, signs and wonders, then their genuine spiritual faith will soon be weakened and undermined. They will become dependent on these manifestations just as many people in our modern society become dependent on antidepressant drugs. God uses his Word, not signs and wonders, to bring to birth saving faith, and he sustains faith by his personal involvement in the life of the earnest, praying believer.

1 Corinthians 1 is a passage which stands against the idea that signs can create or strengthen faith. After repeating that the teaching of the Cross is the power of God, the apostle says – 'For the Jews require a sign, and the Greeks seek after wisdom: but we preach Christ crucified' (vs 22-23). God does not give the Jews the signs they desired (for they would not produce saving faith), nor does he give the Greeks the intellectual flattery which they crave (for that would not stir them to saving faith either). Instead, the presentation of the Gospel will be found to possess all the power of God. The original purpose of the sign-gifts was to be the divine stamp of authentication upon the first messengers of Calvary and their message. Now that the message has long since been delivered, the original purpose has been fulfilled and the sign-gifts have no further role to play. To give sign-gifts a role, charismatic teachers have had to create new purposes, none of which agree with God's revealed aims.

6
Is the Word of God Complete?

WHAT IS THE STATUS of the Word of God? Is it complete or not? Is it really 'the faith which was once delivered', or is it still in the process of being revealed to us? The most serious error of the charismatic movement is that its ideas about prophecy and miracles undermine the very foundation of the Scripture as a completed revelation. Many sincere believers in God's Word have been drawn into modern charismatic ideas without realising that they destroy the exclusive authority and sufficiency of the Scripture.

According to the charismatic view, prophecy, including the revealing of authoritative directions from God, is still going on. According to the Bible, all revelation was completed in the time of the apostles and no further direct revelation of authoritative Truth is to be expected. Here are the passages in *John's Gospel* in which the Lord Jesus Christ emphasised that his close disciples would be led by the Holy Spirit to deliver *all* the Truth, so as to give a *complete*, perfect, and finished revelation.

'But the Comforter, which is the Holy Ghost, whom the Father will send in my name, he shall teach you all things, and bring all things to your remembrance, whatsoever I have said unto you' *(John 14.26)*.

'But when the Comforter is come, whom I will send unto you from the Father, even the Spirit of truth, which proceedeth from the Father, he shall testify of me: and ye also shall bear witness, because ye have been with me from the beginning' *(John 15.26-27).*

'I have yet many things to say unto you, but ye cannot bear them now. Howbeit when he, the Spirit of truth, is come, he will guide you into all truth: for he shall not speak of himself; but whatsoever he shall hear, that shall he speak: and he will shew you things to come. He shall glorify me: for he shall receive of mine, and shall shew it unto you' *(John 16.12-14).*

Scripture is complete, and we are given a solemn commission and trust to keep it that way in the letter of *Jude*: 'It was needful for me to write unto you, and exhort you that ye should earnestly contend for the faith which was once delivered unto the saints' *(Jude 3).*

We are warned in the closing verses of *Revelation* never to tamper with the perfect, complete Word of God. There will be no further revelation. The vision and the prophecy is now sealed up. 'For I testify unto every man that heareth the words of the prophecy of this book, If any man shall add unto these things, God shall add unto him the plagues that are written in this book: and if any man shall take away from the words of the book of this prophecy, God shall take away his part out of the book of life, and out of the holy city, and from the things which are written in this book' *(Revelation 22.18-19).*

Some have claimed that these words apply only to the book of *Revelation*, but this view fails to take account of the same warning in the 'first' book of the Bible (the Pentateuch was originally one book) – *Deuteronomy 4.2:* 'Ye shall not add unto the word which I command you, neither shall ye diminish aught from it, that ye may keep the commandments of the Lord your God which I command you.'

It may be said that the Bible opens and closes with the same warning. With the last verse of *Revelation* the Book of God was sealed.

An American Presbyterian scholar, J. Rodman Williams, wrote the first charismatic systematic theology, *Renewal Theology* (1996). In his book *The Era of the Spirit* he set out the typical charismatic view insisting that God is still speaking through tongues and prophecies. He wrote: 'In prophecy God speaks. It is as simple, and profound, and startling as that! What happens in the fellowship is that the word may suddenly be spoken by anyone present, and so variously, a "Thus says the Lord" breaks forth. Most of us, of course, were familiar with prophetic utterances as recorded in the Bible, and willing to accept it as the Word of God. Isaiah's or Jeremiah's "Thus says the Lord" we were accustomed to, but to hear a Tom or a Mary today...speak the same way! Many of us had convinced ourselves that prophecy ended with the New Testament...until suddenly through the dynamic thrust of the Holy Spirit, prophecy comes alive again.'

Charismatic teachers all claim that their prophecies, visions and 'words of knowledge', though direct messages from God, do not undermine Scripture because all of them must be tested by the Scriptures. But the simple fact is that countless prophecies and visions 'received' by charismatic believers are never tested by the Bible, and yet are acted upon and obeyed. Indeed, vast numbers of revelations are received which *cannot* be so tested because they are about current affairs in the believer's church or circle. How can a message be tested when it accuses someone of insincerity, or declares that someone will recover from a very ordinary illness?

Even where modern prophecies are simply restatements of biblical Truth, they undermine the Scripture, for God has said that the Bible is the sole vehicle of revelation, and it is completely sufficient for all our needs. God's people should not be trained to accept other voices that claim inspiration. God has said that there will be no more Truth revealed by direct messages or voices on occasions when we need guidance, comfort or encouragement. We will not be provided with extra revelation of any kind, for we are to use the doctrines, promises and comforts already revealed in the Scripture to guide us in every case.

It is not good enough for charismatic teachers to say that their 'extra' messages do not actually contradict the Bible. They certainly undermine the Scripture by providing an alternative fountain of 'inspired' light and help, taking believers away from the one source of objective Truth. The Lord has spoken to us clearly through Paul in *Romans 15.4* – 'For whatsoever things were written aforetime were written for our learning, that we through patience and comfort of the scriptures might have hope.'

The fact is that charismatic teachers do not grasp that the Scriptures are (a) complete, (b) totally sufficient for all our needs, and (c) deep and profound enough for every possible problem and situation. Whether they have done it deliberately or not, they have joined the ranks of heretics in downgrading the Word of God. The Roman Catholic Church has added to the Bible by trusting her own church traditions and leaders as authoritative. Liberal theologians have placed their reason and the science of the day on a par with Scripture. Heretical 'pietistic' movements have put their own 'inner light' on the same level as Scripture – and that is exactly what countless charismatic leaders do to an ever-increasing extent.

The Scriptures are complete, and, as the three major confessions of faith of the seventeenth century put it, 'Nothing at any time is to be added whether by new revelation of the Spirit, or tradition of men.' Today we must reject absolutely the charismatic mania for supplementing it with prophecies, tongues, interpretations, visions and experiences.

The completing of the New Testament was part of the 'foundation stage' of the Church, and special revelational gifts (apostles and prophets) were given to the Church for this period. Once the Word of God was complete the foundation stage was over, and the revelational gifts were no longer given. Consider for a moment the biblical description of this foundation stage.

The apostles performed sign-miracles in order to establish that the Messiah had come, and had revealed his Word to them. Thus, in *Ephesians 2.19-20* we read – 'Now therefore ye are no more strangers and foreigners, but fellowcitizens with the saints, and of the household of God; and are built upon the foundation of the apostles and prophets, Jesus Christ himself being the chief corner stone.'

We note that the Church is here said to have been built, not on the foundation of Jesus Christ, but on the 'foundation of the apostles and prophets'. Of course, Christ is the true foundation of the Church, for 'other foundation can no man lay than that which is laid, which is Jesus Christ.' But another foundation – the apostles and prophets – is also described for one very good reason. Let us remember that Jesus Christ, who died as our substitute, and is the Author of our faith, did not write one word of the Bible. We would never know anything of what he did on that cross, nor would we have heard of the empty tomb and the resurrection, but for the function uniquely performed by the apostles and prophets. From a revelatory standpoint, all we know about God and his beloved Son and the true Gospel comes uniquely through the apostles and prophets of Bible times.

The Lord Jesus Christ is the chief cornerstone, but apostles and prophets, by inspiration, wrote the entire New Testament. Two apostles and two prophets wrote the four Gospels; the two apostles were Matthew and John and the two prophets were Mark and Luke. What is the difference between these two kinds of inspired person? The apostles were men who were chosen by God to walk with Jesus in his public ministry for three-and-a-half years and, in the case of some of them, to have special revelation to write Scripture. Prophets were men who had not necessarily walked with Jesus, but who also received messages from God, some receiving special revelation to write Scripture. (Their inspired writings were authenticated by apostles.)

The whole of the New Testament was written by these apostles and prophets. There were apostles such as Peter, John and the special apostle Paul, and prophets such as Luke (who wrote *Acts*) and James and Jude, half-brothers of Jesus, plus the author of *Hebrews*. The Saviour, although the ultimate author, did not himself write one word. This group of apostles and prophets is a limited, special, chosen group that constituted the revelatory foundation of the Church in Holy Scripture. There can be no more of them for they are the foundation. A building can have only one foundation, and this must be fixed, stable, complete and secure before the building is erected. Therefore, there can be no other apostles and prophets besides those who are called in Scripture – 'the foundation'.

Paul was a special apostle prepared by God to provide a bridge from the Israelite apostles who walked with Jesus, to the Gentile world. In *1 Corinthians 15* Paul says that the risen Lord Jesus was seen by all the apostles – 'and last of all he was seen of me also, as of one born out of due time.' Paul indicates here that he was the last apostle – there were no more. Today, the complete and finished character of revelation is not honoured or protected by those in the charismatic and similar movements. Their attitude runs something like this: 'This is unacceptable! I want to be a prophet. Why say that God only revealed his Truth through them? I have equal, if not greater faith. I believe I too am a channel of new revelation, a spokesman, a voice, a mouthpiece for God. I want divine words to come from my tongue.'

The only biblical response to this is to say – 'You may not have that privilege. You have not been specially chosen by Christ to be part of the foundation of his Church. The foundation has long since passed. You live in the superstructure phase of church history. You can never have special revelatory privileges. It has nothing to do with whether God has the power to do it, or whether you have the faith to receive it. It is all to do with the fact that God has not planned that his Church should have 14, 15 or 20 different foundations, or 75 or 156 different apostles and prophets. There are no more apostles and prophets.'

How thrilled and thankful we should be for the privileges which our God has given us. We should not want or demand illegitimate privileges. We should not want to twist and misrepresent God's Truth in order to have experiences which he never intended us to have in this phase of the history of his Church.

Even within the lifetime of the apostles, as the completion of the Scriptures drew near, there are indications that their power to work sign-miracles was being withdrawn. Take the example of Paul. It would appear that the last sign-miracle of healing he ever experienced was when he cast off a deadly poisonous serpent on the island of Malta. That occurrence astonished the inhabitants of that small island and attracted attention to Paul's divine authority as an apostle. As far as we can tell, however, it was his last healing experience, because he subsequently wrote letters which included statements like these:–

First, to Philippi, his favourite church: 'Yet I supposed it necessary to send to you Epaphroditus, my brother, and companion in labour, and fellowsoldier, but your messenger, and he that ministered to my wants. For he longed after you all, and was full of heaviness, because that ye had heard that he had been sick. For indeed he was sick nigh unto death: but God had mercy on him.' Now this illness of Epaphroditus was a very long one, yet there is not one hint that Paul healed him. How could his illness have been prolonged if Paul had still possessed the power of instantaneous, supernatural healing?

And then Paul wrote in his last letter, *2 Timothy*, these words: 'Trophimus have I left at Miletum sick.' Why did he do that? If he had the power to heal him, why did he not do so? The implication is that he could not heal him. In fact Paul said to Timothy: 'Drink no longer water, but use a little wine for thy stomach's sake and thine often infirmities.' Do we understand what this implies? The foundation of the Church was now in the final stages of completion.

Some have suggested that by the time AD 70 arrived, which Paul never lived to see, the whole problem of tension with Israel ended with the destruction of the Temple, and so the sign-miracles of the apostolic era ended. Whether or not this was the precise moment of their withdrawal, Paul did not have to wait until AD 70. He experienced the scaffolding of the foundation of the Church being removed. As the inscripturated revelation upon which the Church of Christ would be built drew to completion, the signs abated. It is entirely probable that John, the last survivor of the apostles, never experienced in his later life any more sign-miracles of healing.

Because we have the Saviour's express words to the effect that *all* the Truth would be committed to the disciples, and because the revelatory gifts are described by Paul as foundational, we must never add to, or subtract from, the Word of God as it stands revealed. Every word of God is pure, says *Proverbs 30.5-6* – 'Add thou not unto his words, lest he reprove thee, and thou be found a liar.'

If we add anything to what God has said, he will add to us the plagues which he has written in the book of *Revelation*, as we are warned in the last verses of the Bible. These plagues are described in *Revelation 6 to 19*. Therefore, we must be very careful to observe the boundary lines of God's revealed Word. He is against our additions, or our adjustments, or our revisions of his revelation of Truth.

This Word is infinitely important, precious, valuable material, and God says to us, as he did to Israel, 'Do not dare add one word to what I have said, because if you do, you will be under judgement.' That is what we must weigh, as we think of the place of 'prophecy' today. What are we doing to God's foundation – to God's apostolic and prophetic revelation? How does the idea that God is inspiring prophets today affect the uniqueness and significance of what God has said in his Word? It destroys that uniqueness, and steals from the exclusive and absolute authority of God's perfect and only Word.

7
Tongues Were Never for Personal Benefit

NOWADAYS, THE PRACTICE of tongues-speaking in charismatic circles is promoted for personal benefit. It is desired as a *personal* sign, and for its supposed spiritual, emotional and ecstatic value in private devotions. But this is due to a failure to grasp the plain teaching of the New Testament that *all* the sign-gifts of the foundation stage of the church were designed to benefit the whole church. Tongues were never intended for the subjective and personal benefit of the tongues-speaker. *1 Corinthians 12.7* makes this clear, 'But the manifestation of the Spirit is given to every man to profit withal.' Perhaps modern translations make it clearer. The *NASB* reads, 'But to each one is given the manifestation of the Spirit for the common good.' 'The common good' is a phrase also employed by the *ESV* and *NIV*. The *MLB* says 'the common welfare'.

The principle should be learned by charismatic believers: each gift was given to benefit in some way the *whole church*, not just the individual who possessed the gift. This benefit could be to the local church or the church at large. Apostles, for example, were not present in the vast majority of local churches, but their inspired teaching benefited all believers everywhere. Because tongues-speaking was meant as a sign to unbelieving Jews (as Paul clearly states in *1 Corinthians 14.21-22*), it validated the new Christian church in their eyes, and therefore it was an enormous benefit to many. In addition the actual message which came via the tongues-speaker was an inspired word from God which taught and benefited the congregation which heard it. It was certainly a rather cumbersome form of prophecy, for it required translation, and for this reason it was inferior to straightforward prophecy. Nevertheless, the message was a real word from God to the assembled believers, and the tongues-speaker was therefore a type of prophet. He would bring vital inspired teaching for the benefit of all who heard, until the Scriptures were complete, then he would be redundant. Where, then, do charismatic teachers find their authority for the private use of tongues either as a prayer language or for personal upbuilding? The answer, amazing as it may seem, is that they take their authority from a passage which really states the opposite – *1 Corinthians 14.2-20*.

The passage begins with the words – 'For he that speaketh in an unknown tongue speaketh not unto men, but unto God: for no man understandeth him; howbeit in the spirit he speaketh mysteries.'

The purpose of this verse is to show the pointlessness of tongues-speaking if it is not understood by the people listening. To speak words which they cannot understand means that God is the only listener, and that is pointless because God gave the words in the first place (see *Acts 2.4*).

The tongues-speaker of *1 Corinthians 14.2* clearly received a message from God which he understood, for Paul goes on to say that he edified himself, which was not the purpose of the gift. It was intended for the common good. It would appear that sometimes Corinthian tongues-speakers were not troubling to translate their messages into Greek, and so the apostle shows them the absurdity of their omission. If God gave the messages in the first place, he argues, and the tongues-speaker is edified, yet fails to translate them for the church, then God himself ends up as the only listener. The tongues-speaker *must* interpret so that the church may be edified (see *1 Corinthians 14.5*).

Charismatic teachers also pluck out of context *1 Corinthians 14.4* to support the idea of private tongues-speaking. Here Paul says, 'He that speaketh in an unknown tongue edifieth himself.' However, Paul is not justifying 'selfish' tongues-speaking, but as we have seen, he is dealing with the great mistake of failing to translate the tongue for the rest of the people. Throughout his statement he says repeatedly that tongues *must* yield a message for the assembly. Says Paul, in effect, 'Whoever speaks a foreign-language message without providing an interpretation speaks to himself, edifies himself alone, and so misuses the message which he has been given.' The fact that these tongues-speakers were *edified* (which means that their *understanding* was built up) tells us that they definitely understood the meaning of their tongues themselves. Perhaps for some the possession of the gift had become more important than its purpose.

When the New Testament states that tongues-speaking must *edify* everyone, it disqualifies any uninterpreted tongue which does not lead to the upbuilding of the *understanding*. This means that it is not possible to have the gift of tongues simply as a personal emotional-cum-spiritual experience. Whenever the word translated *edify* (meaning *build up*) is used in the Greek New Testament it is used in a context which has to do with learning some tangible truth, dispelling all mystery, superstition or confusion. Edification may be accomplished by words of instruction, encouragement or testimony, or even by the power of example, but in every case a definite and describable lesson is received by those who benefit, so that their understanding is built up. Beyond all controversy it means – to build up the understanding. (See *Romans 14.19; 15.2; 1 Corinthians 8.1; 10.23; 14.3* and *12; 2 Corinthians 10.8; 12.19; 13.10; Ephesians 4.12-16; 1 Thessalonians 5.11; 1 Timothy 1.4-5.*)

Charismatic teachers make another colossal mistake about *1 Corinthians 14.13-14.* They think Paul sanctions the idea that one may speak and even pray in a tongue without understanding it: 'Wherefore let him that speaketh in an unknown tongue pray that he may interpret. For if I pray in an unknown tongue, my spirit prayeth, but my understanding is unfruitful.' These words show, of course, that a genuinely inspired tongue must be understood by the speaker.

How could it be that a tongues-speaker did not know the meaning of his words? It is likely that the apostle here deals with the case of a man who has received a foreign-language message on previous occasions, where he has understood the meaning, and an interpreter has confirmed the meaning. One day, in the course of public worship, while filled with love and praise to God, he feels a strong inclination to 'give utterance' in his God-given language, but on this occasion the words are not accompanied by any understanding of their meaning. (Someone who often spoke in tongues may well have remembered many words or phrases of his language(s), and when filled with a strong desire to be used by God to bring a message to the congregation, some of these phrases may have involuntarily crowded into his consciousness.) If, however, he is given no understanding of the meaning of the words, he is evidently not currently inspired by the Spirit, because tongues-speaking, like praying and singing, must involve the understanding. Though the foreign words jostle in his mind, straining to be set free, on this occasion they have no form or meaning, because the Lord is not behind them. In these circumstances he must not speak out. The command of the apostle to a tongues-speaker in this predicament is to pray for an utterance which carries a clear message with it *(1 Corinthians 14.13)*. The apostle insists that the understanding must be fruitful.

There is yet another verse in *1 Corinthians 14* claimed by charismatic teachers as saying that people may speak and pray in tongues privately. It is *1 Corinthians 14.28:* 'But if there be no interpreter, let him keep silence in the church; and let him speak to himself, and to God.'

As any careful reader will realise, the apostle cannot be sanctioning the private use of tongues-speaking. He would never contradict his earlier statements that tongues, like all gifts, are for the benefit of the whole church, and are therefore useless unless they are interpreted. The charismatic interpretation of this verse sweeps away everything Paul has previously said. Here Paul deals with the need for every tongues message to be *validated* by an interpreter. (This is completely disregarded by charismatics today.) A tongues-speaker with a genuine message from God would utter his words first to an interpreter, together with his own understanding of them. On this occasion the interpreter cannot agree on the meaning and so the speaker must remain silent.

The message lacks corroboration. The instruction that he must speak to himself and to God means that he must subdue his disappointment, let his message speak to himself, and pray. If the interpreter cannot corroborate, then the tongues-speaker is mistaken in believing he had an inspired message.

Thus God provides a double-check on all tongues-speaking. First, the speaker must understand his tongue himself and then an interpreter must confirm that the same sense has been given to him also. This provision completely eliminates the possibility that a tongues-speaker may be mistaken and imagine a meaning for his tongue. Even a godly man may well get carried away and make such a mistake. This 'dual interpretation' arrangement confirmed to the sceptical Jewish hearers that the gift was an undeniable miracle, and assured Gentile believers that the message was truly from God.

The practical matter of how the tongues-speakers collaborated is probably explained in *1 Corinthians 14.28-30*, where we are given the impression that all the prophets (which presumably included the tongues-speakers) sat together. There would not have been many of them in the church at Corinth (we remember the small number of prophets at Antioch, *Acts 13.1*, who numbered five or fewer). Such a small number would have been able to consult very easily before or during the meeting.

If no interpreter is inspired to corroborate a tongue, then the speaker is commanded to speak to himself, and to God, which does not mean that he engages in private tongues-speaking for his own benefit, or in his personal devotions. It means that he is to apply his message to his own soul and pray to God to use him another time, in his sovereign will and pleasure. In other words, he holds his peace and submits to the overruling will of God. In the absence of an inspired interpreter he is not authorised to speak. Paul's teaching is that all genuine tongues channel a message to the congregation. Their meaning will be understood both by the speaker and by an authenticating interpreter.

If these requirements cannot be met, the tongues-speaker must be silent and pray to God for leading. The private use of tongues is therefore precluded by the apostle, who insists that all spiritual gifts must

(i) result in the edification of the church, and (ii) be a truly supernatural sign, to shock the unbelief of unsaved Jewish people. It is foolish
for charismatic teachers to use these verses as a licence for private and
mystical tongues-speaking.

8
Should We Personally Seek the Gifts?

THE APOSTLE PAUL'S exhortation to 'covet earnestly the best gifts' *(1 Corinthians 12.31)* is used by charismatic teachers to prove that all believers should aim at exhibiting charismatic gifts, but this is the most superficial interpretation possible. Two questions must be asked as we read this verse: the first being – Who is addressed by the apostle? The second is – What are the 'best gifts'? In answer to the first question, the apostle was not speaking to *individuals*, but to the entire Corinthian church. It is the *local church* as a unit which is to value and desire the greater gifts. For an *individual* to be ambitious for gifts would have been wrong, but for the church to desire them was right.

What were the best, or noblest gifts? Were they tongues-speaking or healing? The answer is given in *1 Corinthians 12.28* where Paul states an order of precedence. The first and greatest gift is *apostleship*, and the least gift is *tongues*. In other words Paul told congregations to desire apostleship, followed by prophets, and after that teachers. Here is the verse: 'And God hath set some in the church, first apostles, secondarily prophets, thirdly teachers, after that miracles, then gifts of healings, helps, governments, diversities of tongues.'

Obviously it would be wrong for individual believers to want to be apostles, for they were the men who had accompanied the Lord on his earthly ministry, plus Paul. How, then, could the church earnestly desire the gift of apostleship? The answer is, they were to strongly desire and be supportive of the ministry of the apostles. They were to zealously heed and treasure their teaching, covet their visits and facilitate their journeyings. He did not mean that they should desire to be apostles themselves. In *1 Corinthians 12.28* tongues are last (and least) in a list of eight gifts. They are certainly not among the greatest. Where does the teaching come from that all must covet and desire to speak in tongues? It comes from a rather lamentable misreading of Paul's words.

In *1 Corinthians 14.39*, Paul summarises his teaching saying: 'covet to prophesy' – meaning that they must zealously and gratefully appreciate the ministry of prophets (who were given by God until the Scripture was complete). He does not tell individuals to be ambitious to prophesy, but exhorts the church as a whole to desire and value the prophets that God had given them. The charismatic view of this verse is that each believer should long to prophesy, but this is contrary to the biblical teaching set out in *1 Corinthians 12.7-11* that spiritual gifts are dispensed solely according to the sovereign will of God, and are distributed comparatively sparingly (verses 29-30) and not on the basis of spiritual ambition.

The command to covet the best gifts, therefore, is made to churches, not individuals. Tongues-speaking is not ranked with the greatest or best gifts, but is shown to be the least. While it had a powerful 'verification value' in its day, Paul placed it far below direct prophecy, and even below the ordinary teaching ministry. Having placed it last in his list of spiritual gifts in *1 Corinthians 12.28*, he did not mention it at all in other lists of gifts such as those in *Romans 12* and *Ephesians 4*. Yet today, thousands are urged to crave this least gift.

Charismatic teachers nearly all insist that after conversion Christians must seek the baptism of the Holy Spirit as a separate experience, and that it will be marked by their speaking in tongues. Accordingly tongues are sought by many who long for evidence that they have received the Spirit. Not only are tongues no longer real languages, as they were in the Bible, but charismatic teaching has changed them from being a sign for Jews to a sign of a personal spiritual experience.

While it is a praiseworthy thing to desire a stronger spiritual life, the notion that a separate baptism of the Spirit is needed after conversion stems from two basic mistakes in understanding God's Word. The first mistake is to confuse two entirely different experiences of the Holy Spirit – the *baptism* of the Spirit, and the *filling* of the Spirit. According to *1 Corinthians 12.13* all true Christians without exception are baptised by the Spirit at conversion, when the Holy Spirit brings them into the family of the redeemed. However, believers may and must be *filled* with the Spirit repeatedly, as we may see from a study of the 'fillings' in *Acts*. We are commanded in *Ephesians 5.18* to constantly seek the *filling* of the Spirit.

This *filling* of the Spirit is an infinitely repeatable bestowal of enabling strength upon believers, and Scripture does not indicate anywhere that there are any 'feelings' associated with it. It is a practical unction given when we need boldness, fluency and clarity in witness, power for service, or help to conquer sin. The teaching of Scripture is 'one baptism, many fillings'. The references to repeated fillings in *Acts* and *Ephesians* show that they were not generally attended by tongues-speaking. At the end of this chapter we list many texts which show that the baptism of the Spirit takes place at conversion, proving that another principal plank of charismatic thinking is totally misguided.

The second mistake which leads to the idea that believers must seek a baptism of the Spirit marked by the gift of tongues arises from a serious misunderstanding of what took place on the Day of Pentecost. It is imagined that all believers must have their own personal 'Pentecost' in addition to conversion. But on the Day of Pentecost the Spirit of God came down in power on the New Testament church in a once only[*] event (like the incarnation or the atonement), signalling the end of the Jewish church era, and the beginning of the church of Christ.

---

[*] There were three 'mini-Pentecosts': Samaria, *Acts 8.15-17* (although tongues are not mentioned here); Caesarea, *Acts 10.44-46*; and Ephesus, *Acts 19.1-7*, which served to bring into full union with the Christian church Samaritan believers, Gentile believers and believing disciples of John.

At Pentecost God changed everything as he had long promised, inaugurating the New Testament church with a fresh burst of revelation, accompanied by signs and wonders. The new church order would in future be composed of regenerate souls, and under the direct rule of the Holy Spirit of God. Pentecost was a unique and unrepeatable baptism of the Spirit upon the church.

At Pentecost the disciples were all 'baptised' by the Spirit into one body – the true Church of Christ; and since then each individual convert is 'baptised' by the Spirit into the true Church of Christ at the time of conversion, as Paul tells us in *1 Corinthians 12.13* – 'For by one Spirit are we all baptized into one body, whether we be Jews or Gentiles, whether we be bond or free; and have been all made to drink into one Spirit.' Therefore, the instant a person is converted he is baptised into the invisible Church, and may be certain that the Spirit is within him. It is wrong for converted people to agonise for the baptism of the Spirit, because he is already within the true believer. As Paul says, 'If any man have not the Spirit of Christ, he is none of his' *(Romans 8.9).*

In charismatic circles the primary purpose of any gift of the Spirit is to give signs, wonders and private ecstatic pleasure. Indeed, these things have assumed a greater importance than the *fruit* of the Spirit in the life of the believer. The sign-gifts which authenticated the apostles and ushered in the church age have ceased, and it is the *fruit* of the Spirit, or holiness and spiritual fervour, which continues to be produced in the lives of Christ's people.

We have already noted that the fillings recorded in *Acts* gave the disciples boldness, fluency, love and real dedication to the work of God. In *Ephesians 5.18* we are exhorted to be filled with the Spirit in the context of holiness and spiritual deportment. It is by the Spirit that we grow in Christian character, even though we may pass through valleys of hardship, persecution, sorrow and affliction. Charismatic teachers seem to advocate signs and ecstatic experiences as a means of floating across such valleys, but that is not the Lord's way. The Scriptures teach that the Lord will sometimes withdraw his smile, and permit trials to come upon us, for a variety of reasons. We may have to be chastised for sin or disobedience, or need to be given trials in order that we may be taught the ugliness of this vain world, and learn to appreciate the Lord and his blessing.

Equally we may need to be taken through hard experiences to wean us from worldly tastes, or to train up some special quality in us, such as patience or sensitivity. The Lord has much to do in our lives, but if we depend upon the artificial crutches of supposed signs and wonders, thinking that trials and sicknesses are not God's will for us, then the real fruit of the Spirit *(Galatians 5.22-23)* will not be manifested in us.

The charismatic dependence on ecstatic experiences insulates believers from reality, but true biblical teaching enables believers to view all their trials and circumstances spiritually, and to manifest the fruit of Christian character and dependence upon the Lord in them all. The purpose of God for his people is not that they should permanently manifest sign-ministries, but that they should be perfected in holiness to become a wholesome, righteous people, walking in genuine patience, trust, and joyful expectation.

Scripture texts which prove that the believer is baptised with the Holy Spirit at the time of conversion include the following: *John 7.37-39; Acts 2.38; Romans 5.1-5; Romans 8.9 and 15; 1 Corinthians 6.11 and 19-20; 1 Corinthians 12.13; Galatians 3.2 and 5; Galatians 4.4-6; Ephesians 1.13-14; Ephesians 4.30; 1 Thessalonians 1.5-6; 1 John 4.12-13.*

9
Bypassing the Mind and the Word

WHAT HARM can charismatic practices do to believers who take them up? Among the injuries which they will undoubtedly suffer is the undermining of spiritual faculties, especially the priceless faculty of spiritual discernment and understanding. We have already seen that all spiritual gifts must *edify* – a word which the Greek New Testament always uses to indicate the building up of our understanding. All true gifts must instruct the mind. Every word in the Bible is directed at the conscience, affections and will of the believer *through the mind,* and so important is the centrality of our reasoning faculty that Paul tells Timothy that God has given us the spirit of 'a sound mind' *(2 Timothy 1.7).*

We must always respond to God in accordance with the Saviour's principle for worship – 'in spirit and in truth' *(John 4.24).* All prayer and worship is to be understood by our rational minds and sincerely directed to God as a voluntary, conscious act. The mind is never to be left out or switched off. This is an unchanging principle of the faith for Christians. We are not Eastern mystics, but charismatics have slipped into the murky paths of mysticism. They no longer cleave to biblical teaching when they abandon the 'sound mind', or the understanding. Paul says *(1 Corinthians 14.15)* that we must pray with the spirit and 'with the understanding also'. We must sing with the spirit and 'with the understanding also'.

The charismatic pursuit of tongues, prophecies and visions surrenders conscious control of words and thoughts. The intelligent understanding of the meaning of a privately-indulged tongue is zero. According to most charismatic teachers the highest evidences of a believer's communion with God are ecstatic experiences which eliminate the mind altogether, being felt only at an emotional level.

Although such teachers insist that tongues-speaking and trance-like states edify, it is beyond dispute that things happen which the worshipper does not understand, and do not build up his knowledge of the Word of God. Therefore, tested by Scripture, these charismatic practices are not valid worship or communion with God. All ministry and worship must be understandable. It must proceed via the mind to touch the heart.

An emotional high, or 'cloud nine' experience, as sought by many charismatic worshippers, is carnal rather than spiritual because it affects the emotions without involving the mind. In *Ephesians 5.18* Paul says: 'Be not drunk with wine, wherein is excess; but be filled with the Spirit.' Another translation reads: 'Do not get drunk with wine, for that is dissipation.' Being 'filled with the Spirit' is the opposite of being drunk. When drunk, people suppress and disable their mind and reason, but when filled with the Spirit the mind becomes more alive, and God's Truth is wonderfully grasped and felt. The understanding is enlarged, even emancipated. When musing alone, or when doing some menial task which requires no great concentration, Christians may rejoice and worship, singing and making melody in their hearts to the Lord, with 'psalms and hymns and spiritual songs' *(Ephesians 5.19)*, because being filled with the Spirit leads, not to unintelligible languages and ecstasies, but to clear, heartwarming reflection on the things of God.

In *Galatians 5.22-23* the apostle sets forth the *fruit* of the Spirit. Is the mind or understanding bypassed here? Not at all, because every single virtue and Christian practice requires the participation of the mind as well as the heart. One of the virtues listed is *temperance,* or self-control. A believer must never be out of control; never in a 'drunken' ecstasy. Nor should a believer get into any kind of cultish trance-state. A worldling may wish to dull the mental faculties, to escape from reality and allow baser desires freedom, but the Christian, by the help of God, is to maintain understanding and self-control. Many charismatic teachers say the opposite, calling upon believers to break the 'shackles' of the rational mind, and to seek 'liberty'.

The evangelical who becomes charismatic pushes the mind into an inferior place, and so becomes an excessively emotional kind of person. He now assesses things in an entirely subjective way, rather than in an objective and biblical way. For this person, Scripture loses its total authority, so that increasing trust is placed in what leaders say, anecdotes, strange experiences, apparent signs and wonders and personal desires.

An example of the abdication of proper mental control in charismatic circles is the use of hypnotic techniques. The widespread occurrence of people being 'slain in the Spirit' is an example of placing people into a form of trance. Such phenomena used to be the stock-in-trade of the theatrical hypnotist. The audience largely succumbed to the power of hypnotic suggestion by believing the hypnotist's statement that certain things would happen. Even the more cynical people would soon be persuaded once phenomena began to take place. When the hypnotist called for volunteers to join him on the platform and 'commanded' them to display the effects he had predicted, whether falling down at a touch, being unable to move, experiencing deadness of limbs or whatever other effect, they would comply.

This writer recalls seeing such a performance as a boy. The hypnotist lined up a dozen volunteers, seated in chairs on the stage. He told them that they would find their chair too hot to sit on and be compelled to leap up. Once standing, he said, they would be unable to move. Two or three people in particular would then find that the stage felt hot. One after another the volunteers leapt from their chairs with looks of pain, exclaiming that their chairs were burning them. Then they found they could not move. Bizarre effects were commonly achieved by performers who had mastered the craft of hypnotic suggestion. We should not be impressed to read of the hysterical laughing and sobbing episodes, and the falling down, with trembling and shaking, that occurs in charismatic conventions. It is as old as the hills in the entertainment world.

Charismatic healer John Wimber wrote of his encounter with ten German theological students who questioned elements of his teaching. He asked them, by way of experiment, to invite the Holy Spirit to minister healing and renewal to them. He records that they chuckled and said, 'Sure, why not?' To their surprise they experienced extraordinary things which Wimber ascribes to the power of God. He asked one young man, who was rather tall, and standing bolt upright, 'Do you feel anything?' The young man said, 'No, nothing.' Wimber replied, 'That's strange, because I believe the Holy Spirit is on you. Why don't you sit down?' The young man answered, 'I can't sit down. I can't move. I don't feel anything, and I can't move.' John Wimber thought this was the power of the Spirit.

The reality is that there is no such experience in the pages of the New Testament. God nowhere says he will work in this way. But the secular theatre has a long tradition of hypnotists producing identical effects. The New Testament states clearly that in the worship and service of the Lord the mind is never bypassed. The Holy Spirit does not work through hypnotic trances and bizarre, unnecessary phenomena when he brings conviction to a needy soul, or when he empowers a believer for service.

In charismatic healing meetings, forces other than the plain truth of Scripture are used to produce the desired effects. From start to finish a sequence of hypnotic techniques are employed, though often the people using them do not realise they are phoney methods. They simply copy what they have seen others do. An atmosphere of expectation is developed; emotional susceptibility is heightened, and the people are told exactly what 'phenomena' will occur.

As a healing session reaches its climax, the Holy Spirit is 'called down'. People may be asked to close their eyes and claim their healing. The approach chosen may involve the illness being commanded to leave in the name of Jesus. Definite effects will be experienced by susceptible people, but usually these turn out to be illusory or shortlived.

It is not by the authority of the Bible that suggestion techniques are used to heal people or to prove the presence of the Holy Spirit. Charismatic workers may not realise it but they have swerved aside to the ways of witchcraft cults.

The Holy Spirit works by enlightening the minds of men and women, and convincing them of the teaching of the Bible. Only by exercising faith in his promises and power alone do we receive a true spiritual blessing. The Holy Spirit never bypasses the mind of the believer, and therefore any technique or practice which has been devised, such as hypnosis, or subrational tongues-speaking, is entirely of the flesh and not of the Spirit. The mind – which is the rational, thinking faculty – must always be awake and functioning in spiritual things.

There is no doubt that charismatic teaching results in a considerable lowering of the credulity threshold in all its adherents. The most shrewd, level-headed kind of person is unavoidably affected by its 'programming'. A tendency to believe incredible things develops, and spiritual discernment falls drastically. The practice of tongues, the relegation of the understanding to a minor place, the diet of miracles, and the extreme subjectivity of charismatic thinking all combine to produce this inevitable effect. Once people have been mentally conditioned by a charismatic environment, they have been able to take seriously such bizarre ideas as Oral Roberts' claim to have seen a vision of Jesus, 900 feet tall. Charismatic practices loosen up the mind in such an unhealthy way that people will believe almost anything.

Once again we refer to Dennis Bennett, writing of the kind of miracles which (he claimed) are available to Christians today. He quotes David du Plessis, perhaps the best-known 'founder' of the charismatic movement, who tells of a 'miracle' in his earlier ministry, in which he and some others were gathered at a friend's home, praying for a man who was in bed seriously ill about a mile away. 'As we prayed,' said du Plessis, 'the Lord said to me, "You are needed at that bedside right away."' He immediately rushed out of the house, recalling, 'As I took one step out of the gate, my next step fell on the front step of the house a mile away where our sick friend was. It startled me greatly. I know that I was carried that mile instantly because some fifteen minutes later, the rest of the men I had been praying with came puffing down the drive and asked me, "How did you get here so fast?"'

Charismatic books have been crowded with this kind of story. Dennis Bennett recorded how the power and glory of God once lifted an evangelist several feet off the ground in full view of the congregation. Are such reports only foolish exaggeration or hearsay, or are they outright lies of the kind the Bible warns will arise? The charismatic movement certainly prepares the way for the final delusion when 'There shall arise false Christs, and false prophets, and shall shew great signs and wonders; insomuch that, if it were possible, they shall deceive the very elect.' One of its terrifying effects is that it impairs spiritual discernment, making Christians vulnerable to the devil's powers, signs and lying wonders in the final apostasy. (See *2 Thessalonians 2.1-12.*) In the meantime it causes God's people to deviate from the true pathway of worship, evangelism and Christian growth. If people believe the unsubstantiated claims of present-day charismatic leaders they will eventually believe anything. If they believe the ludicrous and extravagant stories of extrovert, spiritually-deluded showmen, how will they stand against the lying wonders to be unleashed during the final apostasy? Will the elect be deceived?

Another serious charismatic abuse of the mind comes in the form of visions and other direct messages from God, which are now regularly claimed by charismatic leaders. Their adherents set great store by such messages. They derive guidance about the will of God from dreams and 'inner impressions', claiming clairvoyant knowledge of other people's affairs and future events. Sincere believers must be warned away from all this extra-sensory perception because it is scripturally disqualified as a source of spiritual instruction and guidance for today, and therefore highly deceptive. Instead of the mind being used to receive and understand God's Word, the imagination becomes a trusted source of direct revelation, and lord in people's lives.

10
Is the Holy Spirit In It?

THE MOST BAFFLING characteristic of the modern charismatic movement is its quite amazing capacity for liaison with outright heresy, extreme worldliness, and criminal workers. Large numbers of charismatics do not seem to care much about the compromise which their compatriots court around the world. When it comes to contending for the faith against Romanism, modernism, ecumenism, occult ideas, this world's Vanity Fair, or sheer fraud, the charismatic movement is at its weakest and most defective.

Some of the largest charismatic organisations are openly ecumenical. Pioneers of the movement (David du Plessis and others) said openly and frequently that they wanted to see the emergence of a united world church under the leadership of the pope. It was their hope that all Protestants and Catholics would be won over to charismatic activities, with the result that they would recognise their essential oneness and the issues which divided them would recede and disappear. It is a fact that world charismatic leaders today seem to have no readiness at all to keep apart from doctrinal heresy and apostasy.

In the light of this, how is it possible for this movement to possess the power and unction of the Holy Spirit? Surely the Holy Spirit is the Holy Spirit of Truth. Where he is truly present there is bound to be great love and loyalty to the Word of God, coupled with determination to safeguard and defend it. Yet the charismatic movement as a whole is undeniably indifferent to the defence of the Bible and its sole authority for the church.

Many charismatic leaders have openly flouted evangelical conversion as the only way to Christ by stating openly that Roman Catholics are truly converted Christians who may receive the gifts of the Spirit *without changing their beliefs.* This is regardless of the fact that they continue to deny justification by faith alone, and other doctrines essential to true conversion. Catholic charismatics believe that salvation is dispensed and administered by the Catholic Church through the sacraments. Salvation for them depends on the mass, confession, and so on. Leading charismatic Catholic authors make it very clear that they aim to strengthen the commitment of faithful Catholics to their sacraments, to the virgin Mary, to the pope and to the Catholic Church.

There are millions of Roman Catholic charismatics (it is claimed more than fifty million and even allowing for exaggeration there must be a vast number). In fact, Roman Catholics account for half the total number of charismatics worldwide. Successive popes have endorsed the Catholic charismatic movement because none of its adherents altered their Catholic beliefs. When some years ago a vast charismatic congress was held in Kansas City with 45,000 participants, a Roman Catholic presided and nearly half those present were Catholics. A sequel congress in New Orleans was attended by most of the major names in the charismatic world, including countless Catholic priests. Of those who registered, 50% were Catholics. Mass was celebrated every day of the congress, and totally ecumenical sentiments were applauded and endorsed by all throughout the proceedings.

We have spoken here only of the heresy of Rome, but there are other heresies also. The Prosperity Gospel movement is an obvious and shocking wrenching of Scripture, and constitutes most of the charismatic movement. Considered as a whole, the movement does not regard the Gospel, evangelically interpreted, as the only way of salvation. Only a minority of charismatics worldwide would understand and uphold the doctrine of penal substitution, which is the essential heart of the Gospel. The doctrinal vagueness and compromise of the majority proves that the Holy Spirit is not the author of charismatic distinctives.

We have already noted that the vast majority of the promoters of extreme Gospel-pop culture are ardent charismatics, as well as devotees of groups on the 'lunatic fringe' of Christendom such as 'Clowns for Christ'. Certainly the most worldly manifestations of evangelicalism in Britain and the USA invariably turn out to be charismatic in viewpoint, as do the very worst of the millionaire 'phonies' who have made fortunes on religious TV shows.

We read of internationally-known charismatic broadcasters using donated funds to build fabulous luxury homes. We see their appallingly impious television programmes, programmes sometimes so carnal in character that one cannot believe that there can be any spiritual truth and conscience in those who produce them. Some have been convicted and imprisoned for fraud. Others who became famous as charismatic preachers have been caught out in sexual scandals. Why is it that such appalling things happen far more in charismatic circles than in any other branch of evangelical Christianity?

It is a telling fact that most of the present-day pseudo-Gospel movements of obviously deluded and occult character are strongly charismatic, manifesting all the so-called gifts of the Spirit. The more balanced and earnest charismatics who make up the serious fraction of the movement can offer no satisfactory explanation of how gifts which they believe are given by the Holy Spirit can be so easily manifested by those who turn out to be crooks and confidence tricksters.

Viewed worldwide, no Christian movement has shown greater indifference to *Truth* and godly standards than this one. Is the Holy Spirit really in all the tongues, visions, and healings? Does the Holy Spirit vindicate and condone the unbiblical antics of so many within the charismatic world? Surely not, for it is not the way of the Holy Spirit to work in alliance with error; to blur the difference between 'saved' and 'unsaved'; to promote ecumenism, or to bless worldly lifestyles. He is the Spirit of *holiness* and *Truth*. Sincere evangelicals who have adopted a charismatic position should be greatly concerned by the flagrantly unscriptural stance of the overwhelming majority of charismatic teachers.

Part II
Answering the Questions

MANY BELIEVERS who are not themselves charismatic take the view that charismatic gifts may be true blessings sent by God to those who have them. They feel that they should not express disagreement with those of charismatic persuasion. Some call themselves *continuists* in their attitude to tongues-speaking and other phenomena. In other words, they are flexible on the matter. This neutral attitude seems full of sweet reasonableness, but it is really an easy way out of a serious problem, for either the charismatic point of view is biblically right, and we all are duty-bound to subscribe to it, or it is a serious mistake, and we should be contending for the Truth.

Besides this, the problem of charismatic penetration of sound churches is very great. For the past thirty or so years, many charismatic people have joined non-charismatic congregations in order to draw them into the charismatic fold, even if this has involved bringing down the existing ministry and leadership, and splitting the church. Churches which have opted for a hospitable, irenic attitude when faced by charismatic 'invasion' have found themselves plunged into untold confusion and deep agony. In addition, charismatics have taken over or deeply influenced many old-established evangelical institutions such as Bible colleges, periodicals, publishing houses, conventions and missions. Every way they turn, traditional Bible Christians are confronted by charismatic influence.

The result is that charismatic ideas have influenced the thinking of many non-charismatics far more than they realise. Many pastors have renounced 'cessationism', the traditional view which says that all revelatory and sign gifts have ceased.* They have adopted instead what has become known as the 'continuist' position, meaning that while they are not charismatic, neither will they affirm that the gifts have ceased. So the door is open to charismatic teaching.

The following questions are representative of those which many moderate charismatics and also many neutral Christians raise when the charismatic movement is under discussion. These cause them to linger in uncertainty, unable to categorically reject charismatic ideas as mistaken and unscriptural.

---

* The term cessationism comes from the seventeenth-century confessions of faith, led by the 1646 *Westminster Confession* (1.1) which expresses the ending of revelatory gifts at the completion of the Scripture, stating, 'those former ways of God's revealing his will unto his people being now ceased'. *The Savoy Declaration* (1658) and the *Baptist Confession* (1689) follow suit.

11
What About the Signs of Mark 16?

These words are appended to the great commission of the Lord Jesus Christ recorded in *Mark 16* – 'And these signs shall follow them that believe; In my name shall they cast out devils; they shall speak with new tongues; they shall take up serpents; and if they drink any deadly thing, it shall not hurt them; they shall lay hands on the sick, and they shall recover.' Is this not an unqualified promise to all who believe? If so, then surely these following signs should be expressed in every age?

THE ANSWER to this viewpoint is that the verses quoted, *Mark 16.17-18*, do not apply after the time of the apostles. They do not apply to preachers and believers throughout the ongoing history of the Church, and this is easily proved. We should be put on our guard by the mention of serpents and deadly poisons. No sensible Christian dares to say that the promise of safety when picking up serpents or drinking deadly poison is part of Christ's commission for all believers today. A golden rule of interpretation is to observe the *context* of any passage. The problem which hangs over these verses is the *unbelief* of the disciples. We pick up the trail in verse 11 where the disciples refuse to believe Mary Magdalene's account of having seen the

Lord. Then in verse 13 we find them disbelieving the two disciples to whom the Lord appeared on the Emmaus road. Then in verse 14 we read of how the Lord appears to the eleven, and reproaches them for – 'their unbelief and hardness of heart, because they believed not'. After this the Lord announces to them the commission to evangelise, which applies not only to them, but to all believers who shall follow them. However, following the commission to evangelise, the Lord returns to the problem of the unbelief of the disciples. Addressing *them* specifically he says that certain signs will follow those of *them* (the eleven) who wholeheartedly believe and obey his instructions. *They* shall cast out devils, speak with new tongues, survive snake bites and poisons, and heal the sick. Signs will follow *the apostles*.

This understanding of the passage is made abundantly clear by the change from plural to singular, and back again. In verse 14 the disciples are plural ('them' and 'their'). In verse 15 they are still plural ('and he said unto them'). In verse 16 however, their converts are singular ('he that believeth'), but in verse 17 the narrative switches back to plural when the Lord speaks specifically to the disciples ('and these signs shall follow *them* that believe'). He is not now speaking about their individual converts (singular), but to the disciples (plural). If any of the eleven disciples failed to carry out the commission with wholehearted belief in the Lord, then they would have no part in the wonderful sign-ministries which were to attend the apostles in the inauguration period of the Church of the Lord Jesus Christ. The final verse of *Mark* records that the disciples did obey, and reaped the promise.

This exegesis of the passage is totally confirmed by the books of *Acts* and *Hebrews* which inform us that the wonders were performed 'by the hands of the apostles' (not by Christians generally). Tongues-speaking certainly went beyond the apostles, but the point of *Mark 16.17-18* is to record that Jesus promised that all the sign-ministries would be enjoyed by the apostles if they renounced all mistrust and cynicism.

To summarise, the key to the passage lies in *Mark 16.14* – 'Afterward he appeared unto the *eleven*...and upbraided them with their unbelief and hardness of heart.' The principal subject is – the unbelief of the eleven, and the Lord's special promise to them if they repent of this.

We must therefore conclude that these words were *specifically* addressed to the eleven, and therefore no present-day believers need feel guilty because they cannot heal the sick, triumph over venomous snakes and survive deadly poisons.

12
Is Not the Command to Speak in Tongues Still Binding?

On what basis can it be said that passages of Scripture such as *1 Corinthians 14* are not valid for our day? Surely Paul's words are still binding – 'Wherefore, brethren, covet to prophesy, and forbid not to speak with tongues'?

OBVIOUSLY WE cannot choose for ourselves which biblical commands are still binding today, and which are not. But the command to honour the gifts clearly applies only for as long as the Spirit gives them. If the sovereign Spirit withdraws the gifts, we must not try to work them up for ourselves by, for example, putting meaningless tongues in the place of the truly miraculous real languages of the early church.

A few commands in the Bible are plainly intended for the transient stage when the New Testament church order took over from the Old. Some commands were temporary. Take the example of Paul commanding the churches to pray for him, that he may open his mouth to speak the Gospel boldly. No one would say that this command remains literally binding, because it applied only while Paul was alive. After his death, we pray not for Paul, but for the teachers who have taken his place as messengers of Christ. Similarly, now that the temporary gifts of inspired apostles and prophets (such as the gift of revelation of Scripture) have passed, we must earnestly desire the fruit of their work, namely the Scriptures, listening with anticipation to every exposition of the Word which has been fully revealed.

Those who feel they must obey the command to speak in tongues today face several problems. Why is no one today speaking in real languages, as they did in New Testament days? And what about the great omission in God's Word? For example, where are the instructions for approving, appointing or recognising apostles, prophets and tongues-speakers in the ongoing church? There are very clear instructions and examples of how to appoint pastors, teachers, elders and deacons, together with detailed descriptions of their qualifications, but there is not a word in the New Testament about the qualifications and appointing of the former group.

Outside the *Acts of the Apostles* and *1 Corinthians* there is no mention whatsoever of tongues-speakers. Equally, outside these books the only references to New Testament prophets are in *Ephesians*, and here they are firmly described as being part of the foundation stage of the Church. We therefore believe that the scriptural command to seek the sign-gifts applied in its literal form only while the Spirit gave the gifts. For as long as the prophets spoke, their ministry was to be desired and valued. During the period when genuine foreign-language gifts were given, the Spirit was not to be quenched. But the command ceases to be relevant the moment the Holy Spirit withdraws the special gifts.

This does not mean that *1 Corinthians 14* is an irrelevant chapter as far as we are concerned. Not only is it highly important for us to know that the special gifts of early days were exercised within a framework of order, but we are given in this chapter other vital instruction on the *principles* of Christian worship for all time. Once the sign-gifts have ceased, the *principles* of edification, peace (ie: a harmonious service), the rule concerning women, and the command that all things be done properly and in an orderly manner, will continue to be binding *(1 Corinthians 14.26, 33, 34, 40)*. Oddly enough, these are principles and rules which are disregarded in so very many charismatic gatherings.

13
Why Should Extremists Discredit the Gifts?

Should we turn our backs on the charismatic movement because there are extremists? Why should the doubtfulness of some charismatic claims, and the unsoundness of some teachers, be allowed to discredit the whole? The devil can imitate all gifts, but surely this should not lead us to deny the true.

DOES THE EXISTENCE of counterfeit money destroy the money system? It is true that anything of value is likely to be counterfeited, but this should not be too quickly used to defend supposed gifts of the Spirit today. After all, the original gifts were intended by God to be very wonderful and impressive *signs*, not capable of being easily forged. They were spectacular. We remember the apostle's words – 'tongues are for a sign'. The apostolic healings also were extraordinary demonstrations of power which validated the apostles as true witnesses of the resurrection and inspired spokesmen of the Lord. These signs were designed by God to be uniquely efficient and effective as sign-proofs. They were not easily counterfeited, unlike the feeble, emasculated versions of the gifts we see paraded today. The Lord intended them to be extremely difficult to imitate by impostors.

In those times people lived in small communities, even a place like Corinth being a very small town by today's standards. Ordinary people who had grown up together and knew one another well suddenly heard people like themselves speaking *real* foreign languages which they had never learned. Foreign nationals present would understand them, and other ordinary people would simultaneously be given the miraculous ability to understand and verify the meaning of the words.

The manifestation of tongues in New Testament times was utterly astonishing and astounding to all. It was unprecedented and wonderful beyond description, a most emphatic and powerful proof of God's presence with the young church. In receiving real languages, the early tongues-speakers possessed a sign which, so far as we know, has never been reproduced in the world since. Glossolalia, or unintelligible words not directed by the conscious mind, has been seen everywhere, but real languages never learned by the speaker, no one claims. As far as the testimony of history is concerned, biblical foreign-language speaking does not appear to be counterfeitable.

Today's tongues, not being real languages, are easily achieved by everyone, from non-Christian cult groups to cynical students engaging in experiments. Is this the kind of sign that God would have created in order to rebuke, humble and convince the unbelieving Jews of Bible times, and to authenticate new revelation? Would the Lord have used a sign which contained no evidence of divine power?

The godly charismatic asks us to recognise his gifts as being better than those manifested by the extremists and con-men of the charismatic movement, as well as those of non-Christian cults. We naturally extend brotherly recognition to every charismatic who is a sincere disciple of the Lord, but we cannot extend the same recognition and respect to his gifts, because they are indistinguishable from those of the phonies. We ask again, is it possible that God would have given signs so lacking in divine power that they would be indistinguishable from counterfeit gifts? A sign is surely like a precious key. If it can be easily fabricated by a criminal it is a poor design.

The original gifts were awe-inspiring, riveting, and not at all easy to imitate. The present-day gifts prove nothing and can be (and are) duplicated with relative ease even by non-Christians. The large-scale occurrence of tongues, for example, among cult groups down the centuries must obviously discredit today's tongues as the rightful successor of biblical tongues-speaking.

When the Lord Jesus Christ, as part of his sign-ministry, cast out devils, he was able to throw down this challenge to his critics, 'By whom do your sons cast them out?' The point was that the Jews could not cast them out no matter what methods they tried. Only the Lord could cast out demons at a word, and thus he employed a sign which no one could copy or counterfeit. It is surely wrong to think that the incredibly widespread presence of counterfeit tongues does not discredit the practice. The true sign-gifts of Bible times were quite outstanding, and not susceptible to forgery.

14
Why Not Return to Early Church Life?

If the New Testament speaks of churches that enjoyed constant miracles and tongues-speaking, why should such phenomena be relegated to the past?

IS IT TRUE that tongues-speaking and healing were the constant experience in New Testament churches? This is a vital question because it is completely taken for granted by most charismatic believers that almost everyone spoke in tongues, and healings were everyday occurrences in the early church. The reality, however, is very different. Only three occurrences of tongues-speaking are recorded in *Acts*, in chapters 2, 10-11 and 19, and apart from the instructions given in *1 Corinthians* (where tongues-speaking is limited to up to three leaders in any service) there is no mention of tongues-speaking elsewhere in the New Testament.

As it was specifically a sign to unbelieving Jews *(1 Corinthians 14.21-22)* we generally assume that the gift of tongues was given between the events recorded in *Acts*, so that other Jews could also have witnessed the remarkable sign of real languages being miraculously shown in the church. However, even this is no more than an assumption, and it is an even greater assumption to suppose that *numerous* Christians spoke in tongues *constantly*. The three occasions mentioned in *Acts* suggest that these were distinctive events. On each occasion some special authentication was called for to support the message preached. Each case involved Jews who needed to see that the old Jewish order had been terminated, and that Jews and Gentiles were now together in a new church, ruled directly by the Holy Spirit. The tongues-speaking incident of *Acts 10* is an example.* Peter had just been shown by God, through a vision, that he could associate with Gentiles. Taking a band of converted Jews with him he visited the house of Cornelius. God then took him a step further and showed him that Gentiles were his equals in the Gospel. As he preached to Cornelius and his friends the Holy Spirit fell upon them. Luke relates: 'And they of the circumcision which believed were astonished, as many as came with Peter, because that on the Gentiles also was poured out the gift of the Holy Ghost. For they heard them speak with tongues, and magnify God. Then answered Peter, Can any man forbid water, that these should not be baptized, which have received the Holy Ghost as well as we?' And in reporting this incident on his return to Jerusalem, Peter is very precise, and says, 'The Holy Ghost fell on them, as on us at the beginning' *(Acts 10.45-47* and *11.15).* Peter's language indicates that tongues-speaking had not occurred in Jerusalem since Pentecost.

The only other record of tongues-speaking in *Acts* occurs in *Acts 19.6.* Here Paul found twelve Jewish people who were devout believers in the message of John the Baptist. They had a sincere (but pre-Christian) hope in the Messiah. When they gladly embraced the full understanding of the Gospel, Paul laid his hands on them and they spoke in tongues and prophesied. God gave them a kind of 'mini-Pentecost'. Being disciples of John they had needed to be brought up to date on Calvary and the resurrection. Then, as Jews they needed to learn (like Peter and the Jews of Jerusalem) that a totally new order had come in, and a new church had been inaugurated under the rule of the Holy Spirit. Once again,

---

* The purpose of this tongues manifestation was to unlock the minds of converted Jews to the fact that Gentiles could be true converts and fellow members in Christ.

therefore, there were special grounds for their mini-Pentecost, fully in accordance with Paul's teaching that tongues are primarily a sign for the Jews. Believers today should not be swept away by the charismatic idea that tongues-speaking was an everyday and normal feature of the life and worship of the New Testament churches. Anyone and everyone, it is claimed, used tongues publicly and privately, but this concept is simply not in line with the facts of the *Acts* record, as any reader can see.

The church at Corinth was blessed with a number of tongues-speakers, but an absolute maximum of three tongues messages were permitted in any service, and these had to be verified by interpreters. The speakers were authorised teachers in the church, and women were not permitted to participate. The popular charismatic idea of constant tongues simply cannot be reconciled with the information provided in the Bible.

The same is true for the healing miracles of the early church, for once again a major discrepancy has arisen between the record of the Bible and charismatic imagination. Healing acts were certainly numerous and spectacular, but according to Scripture they were carried out exclusively by the apostles and three named close assistants, and no one else.[*] Paul states plainly that healing miracles were 'signs of an apostle'. Because he did these things, believers at Corinth and elsewhere could be sure that he was a true apostle. He reminds them of this in *2 Corinthians 12.11-12* – 'In nothing am I behind the very chiefest apostles...Truly the signs of an apostle were wrought among you...in signs, and wonders, and mighty deeds.'

If ordinary (uninspired) pastors and church members had been able to perform healings, then there would have been no distinctive authentication for the apostles, yet this was vital, for they were the key witnesses to Christ's resurrection and the penmen (and authenticators) of the New Testament. We can be certain, therefore, that the mighty sign-healings of those days, however numerous, were confined to the apostles and those who they expressly nominated.

---

[*] Ananias, who was directed to restore the sight of Paul, is not said to have carried out any other healings. See chapter 21 for more information on whether others healed.

Tongues and healings were not therefore widely practised by ordinary believers as most charismatic teachers assume. Judging from all but one of the epistles, it would seem that churches in most cities never experienced tongues-speaking at all. Evidently this sign to the Jews was not necessary in every place. Charismatic teachers and writers assume a picture of the early church constantly engaged in signs, wonders and tongues, but this bears no relation to the real facts of the biblical record. It is nothing more than fantasy and illusion.

15
Does God Not Heal Today?

Are not the healing miracles of Christ and his apostles intended as a pattern for the kind of things which present-day churches ought to be doing? Is there no ministry of divine healing for today?

GOD OFTEN HEALS people from their sicknesses, but we must understand that there are two different kinds of healing in God's dealings with mankind. There were once those spectacular, undeniable, sign-miracle healings, which had a specific purpose. Their purpose was to confirm the authenticity of a messenger from God. But there is also another kind of healing which has nothing to do with signs, or the authentication of anyone. *James 5.14-16* describes this other kind of healing – 'Is any sick among you? *[The Greek word implies very, very sick.]* Let him call for the elders of the church; and let them pray over him, anointing him with oil in the name of the Lord: and the prayer of faith shall save the sick, and the Lord shall raise him up ... pray one for another, that ye may be healed.'

We are not told by James to call for a 'gifted' healer, but to call for the appointed elders of our church, godly men from the same local body of believers who know and love us, and they will pray. Then God in his sovereignty, according to his will, not according to our will, will determine how, when, where or whether the sick Christian will become better. Notice carefully, that the passage does not say how the sick person shall be raised up. It does not say how long it will take. It does not say whether or not medicines will be needed, or nurses, doctors, hospitals, or convalescence.

The question may be asked – If the person is raised up, how do we know God did it? We know because this healing is a family affair within and among God's people. It is not for show; it is not a sign to the world. It does not need to be 'undeniable'. It is something within the body of Christ for the encouragement of God's people.

There is nothing in *James 5* which has anything to do with sign-miracles or gifted healers. The passage does, however, teach us that God is aware of, and concerned about, and involved in, sickness among his people, and it gives his prescribed way to cope with this problem.

As we look at *James 5*, with its gracious possibilities for healing in answer to prayer, let us remember that the outcome is in accordance with the sovereign will of God. We must bear in mind that the New Testament is filled with examples of great and godly men who prayed earnestly for physical healing but did not receive it. Take the apostle Paul. Surely, without controversy, he was one of the greatest Christians who has ever lived since the Day of Pentecost, yet Paul was constantly afflicted with physical limitations. He suffered that thorn in the flesh (how we would like to know what it was). But God does not want us to know so that we can more easily substitute our own physical handicap for Paul's example.

What did Paul do about his thorn? He did the right thing. He did not demand a healing from God, nor did he use God's special sign-gift which he possessed as an apostle to heal himself. He just prayed earnestly, in faith, to the Lord Jesus Christ, the sovereign Head of the Church, 'Lord, remove this thorn from my flesh; it is painful; it is inconvenient; it is hindering to my ministry. Please remove the thorn.'

However, nothing happened, though he prayed on three distinct occasions. What was God's answer? 'My grace is sufficient for thee.' Paul's response was – 'Most gladly therefore will I rather glory in my infirmities, that the power of Christ may rest upon me . . . for when I am weak, then am I strong.'

Here is the paradox of all Christian life and ministry: when we are helpless, when we are at our worst, when we have nothing in ourselves to depend upon, then the Lord Jesus Christ can manifest in a unique way that it is he who does the work. 'Apart from me' – he said – 'you can do nothing.' Our health, strength and vigour do not provide the effective means by which God will build his church.

What a devastating blow Paul's infirmity is to the theology of the modern faith-healing movement which claims that our physical ailments are an exact measurement of our *lack of faith* in Jesus Christ's atoning work, which, they say, provided for our healing. The greatest saints in the history of the Church include many who have been helpless, hopeless cripples, and blind saints who have never been healed. The case of Joni – a young lady in the United States who was paralysed from the neck down – is now well known. For a brief season, as you read in her remarkable book, she was led to believe that by faith she could be instantly healed. This was one of the most tragic periods of her life, and she discovered from a careful, prayerful study of Scripture that the idea was a total deception.

In the light of *Acts 19*, we may say that the apostle Paul was an expert at healing people supernaturally. On the basis of this, many charismatic faith-healers in America will appeal on their TV programmes for portions of garments to be sent to them, preferably with some money attached! The garment will be prayed over and sent back to the sender (without the money) and healing will be guaranteed, subject to this qualification – your healing will be accomplished in proportion to your faith. In other words, it is not the healer's responsibility whether or not anything happens, and no one will get their money back if there is no healing. What a travesty of the New Testament! What blasphemy! What a perversion of the unique sign-miracle ministries of the apostles!

The charismatic movement has failed to distinguish between the two kinds of healing clearly revealed in the Bible, namely, authenticating sign-miracle healing performed by the hands of temporary apostles, and the ongoing kind of healing described in *James 5*. This is our healing ministry for today, but it is of a quite different style and order from the ministry of sign-miracles.

16
Surely We Must Exorcise Demons?

Demonic powers assaulted the church in the first century and presumably continue to do so in our twenty-first century. In the light of this, is not the charismatic ministry of exorcism valid and necessary?

THE CASTING OUT of demons has been a central feature of charismatic activity, contrary to the clear teaching of Scripture. To begin with, the Bible indicates that since the atoning death of Christ at Calvary, people can no longer be occupied by demons *against their will*, but only as the result of wilful voluntary interaction and co-operation with the spirit world. Thus demon possession has become massively reduced in frequency, and virtually confined to circles of deep occult commitment.

Charismatics, however, see demon possession everywhere, casting demons out of people who manifest none of the symptoms described in biblical accounts of possession. In brief, the biblical case against 'involuntary' demon possession is as follows:

(1) The Saviour taught that his work would bring about a severe curtailment of Satan's powers *(Luke 11.20-22; John 12.31; 16.11).*

(2) Demons themselves were aware of the impending end of their freedom to possess souls at will *(Mark 1.24)*.

(3) Demons are described as being in captivity since Calvary, for Christ has stripped them of their unrestricted power to possess the minds and souls of people *(Ephesians 4.8; Psalm 68.18)*.

(4) No open manifestation of Satan (and obviously demons also) is to be allowed until the end of the age. He must work by secrecy and stealth; by temptations and lies. He is forced to remain invisible in his operation, shut out of the power to indwell a person, until just before the Lord's return. This embargo would be pointless if other demons were still free to become 'incarnate' at their whim in large numbers of people *(2 Thessalonians 2.6-9)*.

(5) The ongoing activities of demons are concisely described in various New Testament passages, and the occupying of souls is not one of those listed activities. They lie, tempt, stir up discord in the church, make war with the church, persecute and constantly seek to plant false doctrines (eg: *1 Timothy 4.1; James 3.14-15; 1 John 4.1-6; Revelation 12.17)*.

(6) We have the record of sign-miracle exorcisms being carried out by the Lord and the apostolic band,[*] but there is not one word of command or instruction addressed to the ordinary ministers and believers of the ongoing church to exorcise demons, because these exorcisms were 'signs of an apostle' *(Acts 2.43; 4.24-30; 5.12; 14.3; 2 Corinthians 12.12; Hebrews 2.4)*. Equally, nothing is said about exorcism in the Pastoral Epistles, or the long passages in *Romans, Galatians* and *Ephesians* which deal with satanic activity and temptation.

We must conclude that any form of demon possession will be a rare form of self-induced human tragedy arising from intense yielding to demonic cult-worship. If confronted with such a case of possession, we cannot exorcise, for we have no such power, but we should follow the principle that only Christ the Lord can free a possessed soul, and urge that person to go to him for release. We can no more expel a demon

---

[*] ie: the apostles and two, possibly three, named assistants, Stephen, Philip and Barnabas.

than we can regenerate a soul. We can *do* nothing, except send people to Christ. Believers should never arrogate to themselves Christ's priestly powers and attempt to effect deliverance. No believer should ever try to personally interact with a supposed demon, for to do so is a grave violation of the command of God which forbids commerce and dialogue with the forces of darkness *(Leviticus 20.27; Deuteronomy 18.10-12).* The apostles had a unique command to act in the stead of Christ, but we of the ongoing church have no such office.

The teaching of the New Testament is that our fight against Satan and his hosts is an *indirect* conflict. We do not touch, feel, speak with, or *directly* engage the enemy, but we fight by using the armour and weaponry which God provides *(Ephesians 6.10-18).* As he tempts us we engage in the spiritual duties which protect us, and we fight back, not by verbally lashing out at demons or addressing them, but by prayer, and also by spreading the Gospel and thus winning over the hearts of men and women.

Charismatic writers say incredible things about demon possession, claiming that demons may enter into people at times of illness, or if abused as a child, or through certain sins being committed, or through fear of an impending trial, or through many other events in life. They claim that possession may be inherited, or even 'caught' by being in bad company. But in all these assertions we never see Scripture credibly referred to, or any biblical reasoning. Charismatic authors just seem to make these things up as they go along, but write with forcefulness and authority. What they say, we repeat, is not in the Bible.

We remember that the chief activity of demons now against the people of God is to infiltrate churches with doctrines of their own invention. What a terrible irony it is that while Satan works unhindered in spreading false teaching, many of the Lord's people are fighting an entirely fictitious battle of 'casting out' imaginary demons.[*]

---

[*] The arguments described here are explained more fully in *The Healing Epidemic,* Peter Masters (Wakeman Trust, London).

17
If Preaching Is Inspired, Why Not Prophecy?

Why deny the gifts of prophecy and words of knowledge to people? Traditional preaching, helped by the Spirit, has always contained a 'prophetic' element – God's message for the present time. What is the difference between this and words of knowledge?

THIS KIND OF THINKING represents a very precarious view of the supreme and exclusive authority of Scripture, and those who feel this way are advised to give much more thought to the great principle of the Reformation – *sola scriptura* – Scripture alone. They may not be aware of it, but they have already absorbed a charismatic concept of revelation, and this is completely contrary to the Bible's teaching about itself as the exclusive source of spiritual knowledge for the church of Christ on earth.

Certainly the illumination and help of the Spirit are essential if we are to understand the teaching of God's Word. But everything which is necessary for salvation, faith and life is set down in the Scripture, and nothing can be added to it. The terms 'prophecy' and 'words of knowledge' as used in charismatic circles mean that special and authoritative spiritual knowledge is directly imparted by the Spirit into the minds of gifted people. Such people receive 'insights' and information which 'ungifted' people do not see. By this the doctrine of private judgement (the Reformation principle that every believer may verify everything by reference to the Scriptures) is shattered. Charismatic teaching, unwittingly perhaps, creates a new, elite regiment of teachers who possess special judgement and revelation.

Whatever they may say, charismatic teachers really believe that the Bible is only *part* of God's communicating process. They think that God uses the Bible *plus* people directly gifted with knowledge and insight. Revelation, they think, still takes place in some measure. But God has given his Word, completed in the first century AD, to be the *one and only objective test* of all our ideas, opinions, teachings, thoughts and actions. Furthermore, he has made it so efficient and plain as a means of expressing his will that all true Christians (possessing converted, enlightened minds) may confidently appeal to its plain meaning as the final arbiter in all disputes.

God has not arranged matters so that we depend upon certain privileged individuals possessing the 'gift of knowledge', who alone can tell us many things, or the Bible's meaning. This has always been the claim of Rome, but never of Protestantism until charismatic teaching came along. For Protestants it is a new and very dangerous form of priestcraft. As the 1689 *Baptist Confession* states –

> 'The infallible rule of interpretation of Scripture is the Scripture itself, and therefore whenever there is a question about the true and full sense of any Scripture... it must be searched by other passages which speak more clearly. The supreme judge, by which all controversies of religion are to be determined... can be no other than the Holy Scripture... and in the sentence of Scripture we are to rest.'

The biblical teacher is someone who explains and expounds the Word of God, not someone who has a direct channel of revelation from God, or exclusive light from God in any form whatsoever. The prophet is in the past; the teacher of God's settled, completed and established Word is God's instrument today. James Montgomery expresses this in a hymn couplet –

> *No need of prophets to enquire,*
> *The Sun is risen, the stars retire.*

This is affirmed by the words of the apostle Peter (written about AD 66, towards the end of the New Testament revelation) – 'But there were false prophets also among the people, even as there shall be false teachers among you ...' *(2 Peter 2.1)*. Here *prophets* are already being replaced by *teachers*, a fact reflected in the Pastoral Epistles which instruct the ongoing church about the appointment of *teachers*, but not about the appointment or recognition of *prophets*.

When a Christian teacher explains anything, he is not *personally* a prophet, but an uninspired representative of the supreme Prophet, the Lord Jesus Christ. Thus no teaching is in the least 'prophetic' unless it is scriptural teaching.

Sometimes, in describing a preacher, people use the word 'prophetic' as a synonym for 'inspiring' or 'apposite'. This use of the word is metaphorical, but it is entirely unacceptable if people really mean to impute an element of direct inspiration to the messages of preachers. The spiritual anointing of a preacher makes him jealous for the glory of God, diligent and efficient in his searching of the Scripture, and probably also forthright, feelingful, sympathetic, passionate and fluent in the delivery of his message, but it does not convey to him special revelation. Therefore the anointing which is sought by the traditional evangelical preacher cannot be used as justification for charismatic gifts of prophecy.

18
Do Not the Gifts Continue Until Christ Comes?

If *1 Corinthians 13.10* ('but when that which is perfect is come, then that which is in part shall be done away') refers not to the completing of the Bible, but to the second coming of Christ, should we not expect the gifts to be exercised until the end?

A NUMBER OF writers who teach that the gifts ceased with the apostles, believe that Paul's words, 'when that which is perfect is come', refer to the completion of New Testament revelation. According to this view, as soon as the Bible was perfect and complete, then the gifts of prophecy and 'inspired' words of knowledge passed away. While we believe this is exactly what happened (see chapter 6), it is not necessarily what Paul refers to in *1 Corinthians 13.10*.

It is much more likely that the term 'that which is perfect' refers to the death of a believer, when perfection starts. (Calvin took this view.)

Others think it refers to the return of Christ, but this does not mean that the revelatory and sign-gifts will continue until then, because the apostle is speaking about the inspired knowledge that revelatory gifts produced. That knowledge was complete by the time of the death of the apostles. Extensive and wonderful as it is, even the perfect and complete

Bible is partial by comparison with what we shall know when the Lord returns, and we shall see him as he is. The revelatory gifts themselves ended once the canon of Scripture was complete, but all that we are given in Scripture will be eclipsed and expanded by the full light of eternal glory.

The idea that the revelatory and sign-gifts will remain in force to the end of the age is a distinctively charismatic view of the passage, not found in mainline historic Bible commentaries.

19
What Is Wrong With Tongues in Personal Devotions?

Does not Paul say in *1 Corinthians 14*, 'He that speaketh in an unknown tongue speaketh not unto men, but unto God'? And does he not add, 'He that speaketh in an unknown tongue edifieth himself'? If, therefore, tongues are a legitimate form of prayer, and also a means of being edified, what right do we have to disparage such a gift?

THIS VIEW of *1 Corinthians 14.2* and *4* misses the whole point of what Paul is saying in these verses. He goes to great lengths to show that tongues-speaking is completely without purpose unless the utterance is interpreted so that all the people can understand. We have already examined this issue in chapter 7, 'Tongues Were Never for Personal Benefit', but it is well worth clarifying the issue further. Paul has already made clear (in *1 Corinthians 12.7*) that each gift is intended by God to minister to everyone, not just to one. (Tongues were specifically a sign to Jews.) Contrary to this principle, some tongues-speakers were omitting to secure an interpreter to validate that their messages were truly inspired before uttering them to the assembled church. Paul is actually correcting such people with a gentle rebuke when he says that they edified only themselves.

As we have noted previously, Paul's words also carry a most important implication which completely invalidates the charismatic use of tongues today. He shows that the tongues-speaker clearly understood his own foreign-language message. Note carefully his words – 'He that speaketh in an unknown tongue edifieth himself.' We repeat that the Greek word for *edify* refers here to the conscious gaining of knowledge. Paul's complaint is that some Corinthian tongues-speakers were receiving genuine messages from the Lord which they understood, and which added to their personal knowledge, but they were not translating these messages and so they were keeping them to themselves. Paul is opposed to this and effectively rebukes them. After all, these messages were not meant for the speakers alone, but for all the church. (See *1 Corinthians 12.7* and *14.5*.)

Today, charismatic tongues-speakers do not understand their tongues. They therefore depend on the interpreter to tell the meaning. The speaker is therefore *not* edified in the biblical sense of the word. He derives no intelligible message from the words he utters. His understanding is unfruitful because his mind receives no tangible instruction unless an interpreter speaks. Therefore, he can never be in the position described by Paul, in which a tongues-speaker, when there is no interpreter – edifies himself.

When a tongues-speaker does not understand his own gift-language, it means that he is seriously mistaken, and his 'tongue' is just glossolalia and not a spiritual gift. We have a duty to protect one another from falling under the power of any experience or influence, including the influence of our own imaginations and emotions, other than that which is intelligible.

'Praying in a tongue' is based on a mistaken view of *1 Corinthians 14.2* where Paul says, 'He that speaketh in an unknown tongue speaketh not unto men, but unto God.' Here the apostle points out that a tongues-speaker who fails to interpret his message puts himself in the rather preposterous and unacceptable position of preaching to God, because only the Lord can understand what he is saying. This ought to raise eyebrows, because the sole purpose of tongues (as Paul keeps saying) is to bring a message from God to the whole assembly. Authentic and legitimate tongues-speaking was a message *from* God *to* people (operating in the period before the Bible was complete). Paul here shows the absurdity of tongues being directed to God, yet charismatic teachers, in their desperation to find justification for tongues today, turn the apostle's words on their head.

Another misunderstood text is *1 Corinthians 14.14* where Paul says, 'For if I pray in an unknown tongue, my spirit prayeth, but my understanding is unfruitful.' Paul does not mean to say that it is legitimate to pray in an unintelligible tongue. On the contrary, he is saying that if anyone receives a message in a tongue which he does not understand, then he must pray for understanding, because *everything* must be done with the understanding. The spirit of a person may long for God, and in that sense he prays, but without meaningful words no praise is articulated and no petitions made. Whatever we do in the worship of God, says Paul, whether praying or singing, must be done with the understanding. Consider the apostle's words:

> 'Wherefore let him that speaketh in an unknown tongue pray that he may interpret. For if I pray in an unknown tongue, my spirit prayeth, but my understanding is unfruitful. What is it then? I will pray with the spirit, and I will pray with the understanding also: I will sing with the spirit, and I will sing with the understanding also' *(1 Corinthians 14.13-15).*

Paul, then, does not advocate the use of tongues in prayer. Rather he shows how absurd it is to speak in a tongue which we do not understand, by showing how foolish it would be if we were to pray this way. What would we be asking for? What would we be giving thanks for? What would we be saying in praise to God? The answer is – we don't know! Thus prayer would become meaningless. And by this illustration, the apostle invalidates any tongues-message which the speaker is not enabled to understand.

20
Are You Saying the Gifts are from Satan?

The question is often asked – If today's prophecies, visions and tongues are not from God, are they inspired by the devil? Surely it must be one or the other. Is this so?

GODLY BELIEVERS make many mistakes, but it does not follow that the devil is directly inspiring them. A believer may take a wrong route on a journey, but no one suggests that the mistake is made by the intervention of Satan. A believer may become emotionally overwrought, hear noises in the night, and even suffer hallucinations, but all these experiences may be explained without supposing that the person has a demon.

Many people who speak in tongues do so *because* they are sincere believers who have been taught (however wrongly) that God wants them to do this. In all sincerity they have endeavoured to obey, often agonising and longing for the so-called 'gift'. Most will have received coaching to help them speak in tongues. Possessing a powerful desire and need to give utterance it is almost inevitable that they will do so, sooner or later.

As far as sincere believers are concerned, tongues-speaking is no more from the devil than any other hyper-excited reaction of the human mind and body. Healings by the hands of faith healers are to be explained in terms of both imagined recovery or short-lived relief due to the powerful influence of the mind over the body.

Nevertheless, while we affirm that the more sincere charismatic believers are not necessarily under any form of direct satanic influence in their mistaken practices, they undoubtedly make themselves highly vulnerable to satanic temptation. Under the influence of charismatic teaching, people learn to trust in ecstatic experiences, impulses, coincidences, and a host of other subjective influences. The devil soon takes advantage of this, and people frequently trust their impulses as the direct guidance of God. Many proceed to receiving all their guidance through dreams, visions, and imagined words of knowledge.

Tongues-speaking, words of knowledge, and all other forms of charismatic expression are bound to lead to a substitution of sight for faith as believers seek tangible evidence of God's presence, rather than being willing to take it by faith. They are led away from obtaining their inspiration and consolation from the Word and promises of God, leaving them at the mercy of subjective impressions. In short, it is an unkind and dangerous method by which to seek true spiritual blessing. We certainly do not believe charismatic manifestations are demonic, but they expose many precious believers to temptations, thoughts and ideas suggested by the enemy of their souls.

21
Miracle Workers Besides Apostles?

What about the seventy disciples of *Luke 10*, Stephen, Philip, and unnamed miracle-workers in *1 Corinthians* and *Galatians*?

IT HAS BEEN CLAIMED that Paul's statement that the proof of his apostleship was his power to work miracles, has been misunderstood. In *2 Corinthians 12.12* he writes: 'Truly the signs of an apostle were wrought among you in all patience, in signs, and wonders, and mighty deeds.' Charismatic teachers claim Paul did not mean that only the apostles could do these, but that miracles were just one of several gifts that marked out an apostle.

Certainly, there were other marks of an apostle, but signs and wonders are undoubtedly named by Paul as conclusive proof, because they were exclusive to apostles. Other characteristics of apostles, such as people being converted through their ministry, or their having seen the risen Lord, were shared by other people, but when one unassailable proof of apostleship is called for, the apostle names signs and wonders, because no one else (apart from two, perhaps three, close assistants) could perform them.

The idea that the apostles were distinguished only by performing more notable miracles than others is particularly far-fetched, for there is no indication of such a thing in the Bible. If others had been able to perform signs and wonders, the people of God would have been reduced to thinking that Peter or Paul *may* have been apostles, because others could exercise all the same gifts. The integrity of the Word of God itself, and which books were genuinely inspired, would then have had no firm foundation, because they would have been written or endorsed by those who *may* have been apostles. (It is noteworthy that theological liberal scholars are the authors who provide grammatical suggestions against the 'apostles only' position.)

What about the seventy disciples?

When the Lord sent out seventy disciples with healing powers to announce the kingdom *(Luke 10)*, did that not show that the gift of healing would be wider than the apostles?

No it did not, because the seventy were obviously sent on a specific mission (like the twelve in *Luke 9*). They were sent to the towns which Christ would visit. Later, just before his arrest, the Lord spoke to the twelve about that mission. Looking back at it as an event of the past, he said, 'When I sent you without purse, and scrip, and shoes, lacked ye any thing?...But now, he that hath a purse, let him take it...' *(Luke 22.35-36)*. The Lord changed his instructions. Those early missions, therefore, of the twelve and the seventy, were for a specific time and purpose. There is no mention of any further healings by the seventy. After Calvary and the resurrection, signs and wonders became the great proof of apostleship, and they were essential to prove the resurrection to the Jews, and to show the church of Christ that those men had authority from God to write or authenticate New Testament revelation. If non-apostles had possessed the signs, how would churches have known what books and epistles were inspired Scripture? No wonder Paul appeals to this one certain sign of apostleship! We must not let charismatic interpreters muddle it away.

But Stephen and Philip, non-apostles, also could heal

Yes, two and possibly three named men also performed signs and wonders, Stephen in Jerusalem, Philip in Samaria, and perhaps (but by no means certain) Barnabas who accompanied Paul. Besides these there are no other Christian healers mentioned in the entire New Testament. (We have not counted Ananias, who was sent on a single errand to restore Saul of Tarsus.)

Stephen and Philip were very closely connected with the apostles and have been called apostolic assistants. Philip went to Samaria doubtless under the direction of the apostles who took oversight of the work *(Acts 8.14)*. The signs and wonders of both would ultimately have redounded to the apostolic band, rather than to themselves. Perhaps the apostles possessed also the power to convey the gift to close assistants (the view of B. B. Warfield), but as we have observed only two (three at most) are recorded as having exercised them.

The key point for evangelical interpreters of the Word is surely to observe the clear and repeated texts that say signs and wonders (after the resurrection) were the special authenticating gifts of apostles. Because there is no contradiction in the inspired Scriptures, the strikingly limited number of exceptional cases must be explained in a way that does not contradict the apostolic prerogative. (The key texts are *Acts 2.43; 5.12; 14.3; 19.11; 2 Corinthians 12.12*. These are pivotal and decisive in understanding all other references to post-resurrection miracles.)

Are there miracle workers in Galatians 3.5?

Galatians 3.5 reads: 'He therefore that ministereth to you the Spirit, and worketh miracles among you, doeth he it by the works of the law, or by the hearing of faith?' Some anti-cessationists have taken this to mean that Paul, who is showing the Galatians the folly of adopting a salvation by works theology, points to the accomplishments of miracle workers in Galatia, and holds them up as examples of those who believe in justification by faith. They point out that Paul speaks of miracles occurring *currently*, and he is not there.

But Paul obviously refers to himself, and the miracles he worked among the Galatians, and deliberately uses the present progressive language employed in the English translation. It is entirely permissible for Paul to speak this way, because although he is not there, he was there very recently and might hope to return. In any case his healings have an ongoing benefit to those who received them and continue to witness to his apostolic authority and soundness. Also, to speak in this way cemented his closeness to the Galatians, showing that their affairs were constantly on his heart. The point that miracles accompany a salvation-by-faith doctrine rather than a works doctrine is well made by present progressive language. Besides all this, the idea that *Galatians 3.5* refers to other miracle-workers resident in Galatia presents a fictitious scene that has no support in the passage, namely that there were two parties in the Galatian church, one sliding into the doctrine of the Judaizers, and the other contending for faith alone, the latter having the miracle workers. The charismatic interpretation of *Galatians 3.5* must be rejected.

Does not 1 Corinthians 12 imply that healing gifts also went to non-apostles?

The list of spiritual gifts in *1 Corinthians 12.7-11* is interpreted by charismatic teachers as though these are given to non-apostles, but the passage does not say this. The intention of the passage is to say that the purpose of the gifts is to benefit the whole body of believers. It should be obvious that the gifts of words of wisdom and knowledge, and of prophecy, would be given to apostles and prophets, and the gift of healing to apostles (in line with other scriptures).

Some have said that *1 Corinthians 12.28-29* separates the working of miracles from apostleship, which suggests that others could do them. But the reason is obvious, because Paul is giving a sense of perspective and listing the offices and gifts in order of significance, partly to show that the teaching offices (apostle, prophet, teacher) are the most significant (and also to show that tongues-speaking is the least of the gifts).

It is a sign of desperation on the part of pro-charismatic teachers that they must search for the smallest hopeful implications in the text that signs and wonders went beyond the apostles. As for the record of *Acts*, there are no instances of signs and wonders other than those of the apostles and just two (or possibly three) close assistants.

22
Conclusion

B Y NOW THERE ARE very many believers who have passed into and out of the charismatic movement. For a time they were deeply affected by the closed-eyes and raised-hands mode of worship, and the uninhibited expressions of emotion in response to (or so they thought) the moving of the Spirit. The experience of worshipping in tongues, 'yielding to the ecstatic flow of heavenly language', appealed to them as a form of 'release'. Eventually, however, they came to realise that the general outlook of their charismatic group was far away from the plain teaching of the Word of God. As they studied the Word they began to be disturbed by the constant flow of prophecies, and they increasingly found the doctrinal grasp of charismatic teachers to be superficial. Many also were shocked by the growing extremism and worldliness of the charismatic movement.

Many former charismatics have spoken of their disillusionment over the lack of real concern for righteousness and holiness. They have found that the 'baptism-of-the-Spirit' formula for sanctification did not really touch their lives and bring them power over their sins. Many have singled out for criticism the charismatic style of worship, with its emphasis on emotional abandonment. With the passing of time they found it all very repetitive, even banal, and it became painfully apparent to them that this kind of worship seldom rose beyond an elementary and highly subjective view of salvation. The overall lack of awe and reverence coupled with the unashamed use of worldly-idiom rhythmic music became jarring and offensive, and their souls ached and longed for something deeper, more substantial, more reverent, more objective, more divine.

A very great cause of dissatisfaction expressed by former charismatics is the incessant exaggeration, seen in the constant claims of amazing wonders, totally divorced from reality. Many who leave charismatic groups profess their relief at being out of an atmosphere in which they developed an almost total dependence upon feelings, experiences, thrills, miracles, impulses and coincidences.

In these days of spiritual confusion, God is calling upon his people to stand fast in the true doctrine of the Spirit – the teaching which has undergirded the worship and witness of Christ's people throughout this Gospel age. At the time of the Reformation, real spiritual power purged many Western nations of superstition and of doctrines of demons, so that people no longer lived in fear of their shadows and in subjection to the fables of Rome. But now the tide seems to have turned and Satan's day of vengeance has come. Through the charismatic movement, the people of Christ have themselves become the advocates of practices often not far removed from witchcraft and sorcery. Never before have Bible-believing people so needed the exhortations of old:–

'Stand fast, and hold the traditions
which ye have been taught'
(*2 Thessalonians 2.15*)

'Hold fast till I come'
(*Revelation 2.25*)

The Healing Epidemic

143 pages, paperback, ISBN 978 1 908919 24 3

Dr Masters here answers the arguments used by healers in support of their methods. He explains Bible teaching on what demons can and cannot do, and how *James 5* should be implemented in churches today. He also proves that the conscious mind should always be switched on for spiritual activities. Included is a brilliant assessment of miraculous healing by a leading British medical professor.

'This volume is a masterful analysis and criticism of the most recent manifestations of charismatic phenomena...The exposition of *James 5.13-14* is excellent, and his analysis of the place of the mind in the Christian's experience is remarkable. The concluding chapter by a medical doctor is also insightful...This is one of the best books on this subject today. It should be widely read by concerned Christian people of all theological persuasions.'
– *Bibliotheca Sacra*

Only One Baptism of the Holy Spirit

109 pages, paperback, ISBN 978 1 870855 17 4

Young Christians these days are confronted by much confusion on the teaching of the Holy Spirit and how he baptizes, fills and anoints God's people. Contradictory statements and clashing ideas flow from a new generation of anecdotal-style books.

When is the believer baptized with the Spirit, and what does it amount to? Is there a second baptism? How exactly does the Spirit witness with our spirit? How does assurance come? Is the believer to struggle against sin, or does the Lord fight the battle for him? What is the filling of the Spirit? Clear answers are given to all such questions, with 'proof texts'. Ideal for all, especially young believers and study groups.

The Personal Spiritual Life

127 pages, paperback, ISBN 978 1 908919 20 5

From the personal indwelling of the Holy Spirit to living a life of commitment these chapters stir and encourage readers to advance spiritually.

In what sense may we 'feel' the presence of the Lord? What was the apostle Paul's method for progress in holiness? How may we identify our spiritual gifts? And how may we count more for the Lord, and sustain spiritual joy?

These are among the themes of this tonic for present-day disciples of Christ.

The Lord's Pattern for Prayer
118 pages, paperback, ISBN 978 1 870855 36 5

Subtitled – 'Studying the lessons and spiritual encouragements in the most famous of all prayers.' This volume is almost a manual on prayer, providing a real spur to the devotional life. The Lord's own plan and agenda for prayer – carefully amplified – takes us into the presence of the Father, to prove the privileges and power of God's promises to those who pray.

Chapters cover each petition in the Lord's Prayer. Here, too, are sections on remedies for problems in prayer, how to intercede for others, the reasons why God keeps us waiting for answers, and the nature of the prayer of faith.

God's Rules for Holiness
Unlocking the Ten Commandments
139 pages, paperback, ISBN 978 1 870855 37 2

Taken at face value the Ten Commandments are binding on all people, and will guard the way to Heaven, so that evil will never spoil its glory and purity. But the Commandments are far greater than their surface meaning, as this book shows.

They challenge us as Christians on a still wider range of sinful deeds and attitudes. They provide positive virtues as goals. And they give immense help for staying close to the Lord in our walk and worship.

The Commandments are vital for godly living and for greater blessing, but we need to enter into the panoramic view they provide for the standards and goals for redeemed people.

Faith, Doubts, Trials and Assurance
139 pages, paperback, ISBN 978 1 870855 50 1

Ongoing faith is essential for answered prayer, effective service, spiritual stability and real communion with God. In this book many questions are answered about faith, such as – How may we assess the state of our faith? How can faith be strengthened? What are the most dangerous doubts? How should difficult doubts be handled? What is the biblical attitude to trials? How can we tell if troubles are intended to chastise or to refine? What can be done to obtain assurance? What are the sources of assurance? Can a believer commit the unpardonable sin? Exactly how is the Lord's presence felt?

Dr Masters provides answers, with much pastoral advice, drawing on Scripture throughout.

For a full listing of Wakeman titles please see www.wakemantrust.org